"The Mission Leadership Team is a book that every church mission leader should read. It is biblical, thorough, rich with helpful resources, and extremely practical. It also reflects changes in the way local churches operate. David's advice will help mission teams of all shapes and sizes to clarify their purpose, stay focused, and efficiently and wisely accomplish their God-given responsibilities. It will cause you to rethink how your mission team is run to make it even better."

      – Bill Bertsche, *Pastor of Global Missions, The Moody Church, Chicago, IL*

"Where does the church in North America fit in this new era of a globalized church? And how do we invite the person-in-the-pew to get involved? In this clearly written guide for church leaders, David Mays suggests ideas and changes for every church family desirous of doing their part in making disciples in all the nations. If you are interested in making your fellowship more missional, read this book!"

      – Paul Borthwick, *Senior Consultant, Development Associates International and author of How to be a World-Class Christian*

"No one in America is more respected than Dr. David Mays when it comes to resourcing the local church in world missions. David's latest resource, *The Mission Leadership Team,* is a helpful, detailed handbook for any sized church to follow in structuring or re-structuring its global ministry team. With great footnotes, appendices, and a clearly laid out format, this book is sure to be the standard for the next decade for any church wanting to energize its volunteer team for mobilizing a congregation in an Acts 1:8 strategy."

      Dr. Monroe "Monnie" Brewer, *President, National Association of Missions Pastors, Director of Church Connections, CrossGlobal Link*

"The local congregation is the foundational means by which the people of the world will be reached with the gospel of Jesus Christ. David Mays has captured for us the relational, organizational, and functional principles by which the task becomes manageable and achievable. These principles, with cultural adjustments, will fit and work in any ethnic context. *The Mission Leadership Team* shows the heart of a Churchman, a missions statesman, and a practitioner. I strongly urge every church to work through this guide, whether participating in missions for years or just starting out—whether re-evaluating or developing a new venture—this work is the guiding tool for which you have been looking."

      – Dr. R. Thomas Cheely, *Missions Pastor at the Briarwood Presbyterian Church (PCA) of Birmingham, AL*

"David has once again pulled together the information all mission pastors need to help them establish a great leadership team, or to confirm that they are on track with what is needed to make their team the best that it can be. I appreciate that he has brought us back to the Word as our plumb line to know we are going in the right direction. This handbook is a must for everyone serving in the role of mission pastor."

         – Liz Gold, *Missions Director at Calvary Church of Santa Ana, CA*

"Most of us serving the church in its mission ministry have had to learn from one another, looking for examples and models from people a little farther down the road than we were. Few seminaries and other formal training institutions offer sound theologically based, yet practical instruction on the task of mission leadership in the local church. Similarly there is a dearth of written resources for such leaders. David Mays has offered in this book a wealth of information and knowledge gained over years of observing and interacting with mission-engaged churches of a wide variety. For anyone desiring to effectively organize and lead a church in strategic mission ministry this book will prove to be an excellent reference manual."

         – Dave Hall, *Outreach Ministries Pastor, Emmanuel Faith Community Church, Escondido, CA*

"David has written a book on what David does best, providing the church with the tools it needs to make disciples of all nations. You will find within its pages the resources and locations of resources to best lead your church in missions. You also will be highly challenged to think through the why, what, where, who and how questions regarding the mission direction of your church. Read it and apply it to your context."

         – Bruce Huseby, *Pastor of Global Ministries, Calvary Church, Grand Rapids, MI*

"David Mays has provided the church with a practical step-by-step guide in setting up a mission leadership team to help guide your church through the process of more effectively engaging in the over-arching mission of the church, namely the taking of the "good news" to every part of the world. This book is full of ideas, helpful suggestions and specific action plans and I am confident that your church will benefit from this much needed resource."

         – Wade Landers, *Global Outreach Minister, College Heights Christian Church, Adjunct Professor of Intercultural Studies, Ozark Christian College, Joplin, MO*

"There is probably no one better qualified to write this book than David Mays. David's twenty-five years of reading hundreds of books, teaching hundreds of classes and consulting with hundreds of churches have given him the platform to write a book that is comprehensive, clear and extremely practical. Every leadership team will be greatly helped in unity, clarity and effectiveness by discussing each topic and then working through the exercises. This is a very valuable resource for newbies as well as those with many years of experience in missions leadership."
    – David Niednagel, *Senior Pastor, Christian Fellowship Church, Evansville, IN*

"Years of experience and great wisdom have allowed David Mays to put together a step-by-step process to evaluate and prepare your mission leadership team for greater, more effective Kingdom impact!"
    – Mike Neukum, *Global Missions Director,*
    Bent Tree Bible Fellowship Church, Carrollton, TX

"David Mays has provided an amazing resource for church mission teams. Few people have the ability to give practical detailed guidance, while at the same time writing about the cutting edge issues in missions. David Mays is not only one of the most well read people I've met, he also overflows with realistic wisdom and helpful resources from years of experience working with sending churches. Thanks David for this remarkable book."
    – Jim Plueddemann, *Professor, Missions & Evangelism, Trinity Evangelical Divinity School, Former International Director, SIM, author of Leading Across Cultures*

"David Mays knows more about how North American churches engage in missions than anyone I know. Every church can benefit from the ideas he presents in *The Mission Leadership Team* and use them to carefully evaluate and improve their mission vision, structures and practices."
    – Bruce Wilson, *Missions Pastor, College Church, Wheaton, IL*

"For many, missions has gotten a little faded and dusty around the edges. A fresh perspective is needed. David Mays' book helps us see how every member (and staff member) has a vital part to play in the Great Commission. By partnering together we can advance the gospel."
    – George Beals, *Pastor of Global Ministries,*
    Central Wesleyan Church, Holland, MI

The Mission Leadership Team

Mobilizing Your Church to Touch the World

David Mays

THE MISSION
EXCHANGE

condeo press
experience the creative power of words.
To order this book please visit www.condeopress.com
CONDEO PRESS was established to allow Christian authors and organizations an
economical and simple vehicle for delivering their books to the public.

This book is dedicated to Tom Telford who has taught me a great deal about churches and missions and has entertained me with hilarious stories from his life experiences.

CONTENTS

FOREWORD

The local church has always been the primary stakeholder in God's global agenda, at the very epicenter of the Great Commission. But since William Carey set sail for India and the Protestant mission movement was born, there has been a dynamic tension, an ebb and flow, between the modality of the church and the sodality of mission organizations.

For nearly two centuries churches were largely dependent on mission structures for information about what was happening around the world and therefore more inclined to express their vision through the initiatives of mission organizations. Over the past few decades, as the world has become flatter and information democratized, churches have felt empowered to pursue Great Commission initiatives of their own, independently. In some cases, churches have chosen to marginalize or even disregard traditional mission structures, taking on the mantle of a full service mission organization within the framework of the local church.

I am seeing encouraging signs that the relationship between churches and mission organizations is moving beyond the bipolar expression of either dependence or independence toward a healthy interdependence. More churches are realizing just because they can become their own mission agency doesn't mean they should repeat the mistakes of the past. These churches are increasingly willing to learn lessons from the overstocked library of trial and error accumulated by mission agency experience.

David Mays has been in the trenches with churches observing this very important season of change over the past three decades. He has been living and breathing the interface of the Great Commission with the local church through his ministry with pastors, lay leaders and mission executives. This practical engagement has been built on an amazingly deep and wide foundation of personal development. I believe I could make a compelling case that David Mays has read more books, interviewed more thought leaders and facilitated more mission-focused webinars than anyone in North America (quite possibly the world) in the past thirty-six months.

All this experience and exposure to fresh thinking about how we do mission has uniquely positioned David Mays to write this book. I have repeatedly challenged him to take on projects like this as a means of stewarding all that God has entrusted to him. I encourage you to engage this resource thoughtfully with others who shape the Great Commission initiatives of your church. If you are not on the mission leadership team (or committee or whatever your church has named this group) I encourage you to get copies of this book for them, or at least pass yours along.

I believe you will find this tool to be comprehensive, flexible, practical and doable. In this short resource David covers all the "big bucket" issues your church will face in sorting out how to maximize your potential for engagement in the Great Commission. But he doesn't try to force you into prefabricated molds of one-size-fits-all thinking. He understands good questions are better than prescriptive answers. As you wrestle with these important issues I believe you will become increasingly convinced there is a practical, doable model in sight that will help unleash the kingdom resources of your church to uniquely contribute to God's global agenda as the primary Great Commission stakeholder He intends you to be.

Steve Moore
President and CEO
The Mission Exchange

October 4, 2010

ACKNOWLEDGEMENTS

This book represents the encouragement, assistance, and knowledge from many sources. Steve Moore, the President and CEO of The Mission Exchange, has been my chief encourager over the past few years. The Mission Exchange Staff are the cheerful, enthusiastic working gears behind all products and services of The Mission Exchange.

My former colleagues at ACMC (Advancing Churches in Missions Commitment) have been an ongoing source of stimulation and information about what churches are doing in mission.

Many pastors, mission pastors, and church mission lay leaders have shared their wisdom and experience through workshops, email surveys, and personal communications. All of you who strive to keep God's heart for the nations in the center of the church's agenda have my highest admiration.

We are deeply thankful for the many people who have financially supported, prayed for, and encouraged us in ministry over the past twenty-five years.

Marcy, the joy of my life, is my biggest source of stability, reality, and blessing.

Jesus – through whom the universe was made, through whom it all holds together, and for whom all things exist – deserves all the honor and glory.

PREFACE

God has given the Church an impossible task. The followers of Jesus are commanded to go into every part of the world—including the most difficult and dangerous parts—to tell everyone the good news, persuading them to repent of their rebellion against the one true God, to accept forgiveness through the death and resurrection of Christ, to surrender their deeply-held pagan beliefs and practices, to become reconciled to God and one another, and to become followers of Jesus.

Friends may consider this task foolhardy. Societies may condemn it as intolerant. The media may denounce it as violence provoking. Governments may forbid it and religions may oppose it because it threatens their control. Extremists may torture and kill to prevent it. And the evil one fights it with supernatural power. It is an impossible task – from a human perspective.

But Jesus gave the command, and along with it he gave his authority, his presence, and his incomparably great power. As this book is going to print, the world has just witnessed the heroic rescue of thirty-three Chilean miners trapped deep underground for seventy days. No effort or expense was spared. God has given the Church an analogous urgent global rescue operation.

The task of mission is much more difficult and complex than the global marketing operation of a multi-national corporation. And the burden for sorting out this complexity, and selecting and undertaking appropriate portions of the task, falls on local church leaders.

Because church leaders are responsible for the "home office" operation as well as local, national, and international "marketing," they often delegate much of this responsibility to a mission leadership team. The team's effectiveness depends on their knowledge, commitment, time, and performance. It is important, but not enough, to love Christ and burn to see his work done in the world. Also required are spiritual maturity, knowledge, and skills in leadership, planning, execution, communication, and cooperation.

This book is intended to help the church mission leadership team acquire and develop the qualities, knowledge, skills, and organization it needs to lead the church in mission. If the responsibilities seem daunting, skip to the chapter on Structure and begin to imagine who can serve on sub-teams and task groups to accomplish the work. If you have multiple teams or a team with sub-groups or separate task forces, you can decide which functions and constituencies belong to each team or group.

It may be profitable to study the book together as a team, one section at a time. If you study and work through each section and incorporate what you learn as you proceed, it may take a long time to get through the book. But it will result in a more effective team that can help your church maximize its impact in the world. And it is difficult to overestimate what God may accomplish in the world through a committed church with good leadership. The potential is enormous!

May God guide and encourage you as you persevere in knowing and doing His will.

David Mays

Note: Because you are reading a print book, you cannot 'click' on the web links. However, you can click on all the web addresses listed in this book at www.davidmays.org/links.html.

INTRODUCTION

Churches have changed substantially in how they operate compared to twenty-five years ago. Larger churches were run primarily by committees of laypeople. The pastor was subservient to a church board. People came to church two or three times a week. Sunday Schools often had larger attendance than worship services. In a strong missions church, the pastor preached a few times a year on missions. Reaching the world for Christ was considered the overarching mission of the Church. Missions was primarily international or "foreign" missions and was carried out by missionaries who were sent by the denomination or by mission sending agencies—often for four-year periods—and supported by many churches. Sunday School classes adopted missionaries, prayed for them, and occasionally communicated with them. Many churches held an eight-day missions conference every year. People were fascinated (or sometimes bored) by missionary stories and pictures from around the world.

The primary responsibilities of most missions committees were to organize and conduct the missions conference and to develop, recommend, and manage the missions budget. It wasn't uncommon for a church to designate twenty to thirty percent of the church budget for missions. Raising large amounts of money for missions was a major annual goal for the pastor and the church board, who worked very hard to promote missions giving. Missions education was conducted from the pulpit through sermons and missionary presentations. The moral and economic decline of our communities and the growth of ethnic minorities had not yet hit the radar screen of most churches.

Today, church life is much different. A great number of churches are staff led. The church board often serves more in an advisory capacity. The church meets once a week. Small groups have replaced Sunday schools. Committees still operate in many churches but are often considered more as hindrances than guiding lights. Many committees have been replaced by "teams" or volunteers who assist staff in carrying out church initiatives. Church leaders still seek to advance the Great Commission but they are much more oriented toward the pervasive moral and social needs of our communities. The scope of the church's agenda has substantially broadened. The need for first-class facilities and multiple staff has greatly increased church overhead and reduced the proportion of funds available to reach beyond home base.

Church leaders still seek to advance the Great Commission but they are much more oriented toward the desperate moral and social needs of our communities.

Missions has changed as well. We can no longer hold to the dichotomy of our nation as Christian and other nations as pagan. Because of the loss of a biblical moral base in our society and the influx of immigrants, our communities have been recognized as part of the "mission field." Church leaders have found it more practical to cast a vision for "mission"—meaning all ministry beyond the congregation—than try to explain same-culture evangelism, local ministry, and cross-cultural missions to congregations that have little "missions" background. Many churches are looking at mission from an Acts 1:8, concentric circle perspective: Jerusalem, Judea, Samaria, and the ends of the earth.

Further, missional churches are not satisfied to exclusively send long-term, church-supported representatives to other nations and cultures. Every member should participate in mission. This often means going on mission trips and getting involved in the community or city. It might mean participating in a church-sponsored project or partnership or volunteering with an evangelistic Christian ministry, a Christian compassion ministry, a community social ministry, or a government-sponsored program.

All of this—and much more—has changed and complicated the job of the mission leadership team. But the first responsibility of any leadership team is to clarify its charter. What is the team's purpose and what is its biblical mandate? What is the scope of the team's responsibility, and what authority do church leaders delegate to them?

FOUNDATIONS
What is our charter?

Purpose

What is the purpose of the mission leadership team? Why does it exist? What is its overall aim? While many things have changed, the purpose the mission leadership team has remained constant: to help church leaders fulfill the purpose of the church. The purpose of every leader, every department and every member of an organization is to contribute to the fulfillment of the purpose of that organization. The team is not an independent group establishing its own purpose separate from or different from that of the church. It is an integral, contributing part of church leadership, pulling together with top church leaders.

This clearly implies that the team is under the authority of church leaders. While the team rightfully suggests, recommends, influences, and urges church leaders to move in the direction they believe fulfills scriptural commands and best meets the spiritual and material needs in the world, in the end, the God-appointed leaders have the final word. The mission team is not authorized to start a rebellion, lead a coup, or take an end run around church leaders.

The mission leadership team exists to help church leaders fulfill the purpose of the church.

The church purpose statement shows what the church is committed to accomplish. The team will have responsibility for the mission portion of that purpose. Examine your church purpose statement to see what portion of it is fulfilled by doing mission. The team will have to identify and perhaps negotiate with church leaders the exact scope or territory of mission, but your team can propose a purpose statement for the mission ministry or the mission team.

It is desirable for this purpose statement to clearly connect with the church purpose statement. When people read both statements, they should see at a glance how the mission ministry fits into, or contributes to, the church purpose. Therefore, the purpose statement for mission might take a form similar to the church purpose statement, zeroing in on the mission portion of it.

Hypothetical Church Purpose Statements and Mission Purpose Statements

Church Purpose Statement 1: *Community Church exists to glorify God by making, maturing and multiplying disciples of Jesus.*

Mission Purpose Statement 1a. *The mission team at Community Church exists to glorify God by making, maturing and multiplying disciples of Jesus beyond our local community.*

Mission Purpose Statement 1b: *Mission at Community Church exists to glorify God by making, maturing and multiplying disciples of Jesus in other cultures and nations.*

Mission Purpose Statement 1c. *The mission team at Community Church exists to glorify God by making, maturing and multiplying disciples of Jesus throughout our city and around the world.*

Church Purpose Statement 2. *Community Church exists to glorify God by making, maturing and multiplying disciples of Jesus in our city and the world.*

Mission Purpose Statement 2a. *The mission team at Community Church exists to help our church make disciples throughout the world beyond our city.*

Mission Purpose Statement 2b. *Mission at Community Church exists to stimulate, disciple, mobilize, equip, partner, and deploy people and resources to make and multiply disciples in other cultures and languages throughout the world.*

Church Purpose Statement 3. *Community Church exists to love God, grow together, and reach the world.*

Mission Purpose Statement 3a. *The mission team at Community Church exists to help our church reach the world.*

Mission Purpose Statement 3b. *Mission at Community Church exists to stimulate, disciple, mobilize, equip, partner, and deploy people and resources to reach the world.*

Biblical Mandate

Whatever the form and content of your purpose statement, it will specifically or implicitly require the mission leadership team to help your church carry out the biblical imperative for touching the nations. What Scriptures guide your mission efforts? What do they call you to do?

The process of working through the Scripture to identify and personalize the biblical mission mandate for your church may have been done in your past and become institutionalized in your

WORK SPACE:

Our church purpose statement:

_____

_____

_____

_____

The purpose of the Mission Leadership Team at our church (my draft):

_____

_____

_____

_____

The purpose of the Mission Leadership Team at our church (approved):

_____

_____

_____

_____

_____

church and in your mission team philosophy and operation. You may have very well understood and accepted biblical principles that guide your efforts. If these are not written out, it would be a good clarifying exercise to write, discuss, and affirm them.

On the other hand, your church may not have carefully thought through this process. You may be doing mission without benefit of a stake in the ground, guiding principles, or strong biblical assumptions. Or your church has changed, and you may need to undertake this process afresh. Who should do it?

In most churches today the senior pastor has enormous influence in the direction and priorities of the church. The input and full support of the senior pastor is critical to any conclusions that will have weight. Perhaps ideally, the senior pastor, church board, and mission team could work through this process together. If it is delegated to the mission team, realize that you must offer your proposals to church leaders and get their thoughtful feedback. The results will have authority and provide concrete guidance only if top church leaders own it.

The input and full support of the senior pastor is critical to any conclusions that will have weight.

You may find considerable help in examining the biblical foundations from other churches, but do not short-cut doing your own Bible study. The foundational study of Scripture will provide you a bedrock commitment to God's heart and desire for the nations.

What Scriptures guide your mission efforts? Here are some Scriptures that other churches commonly build upon.

Great Commission Scriptures:

Matthew 28:18-20   Mark 16:15   Luke 24:44-48

John 20:21   Acts 1:8

Additional Scriptures that Support Mission:

Genesis 12:2-3   1 Chronicles 16:23-24   Isaiah 49:6b

Matthew 24:14   Luke 4:18   John 3:16-17

John 10:10   Romans 10:14-15

Here is a suggested process for writing your biblical mandate statement. Write out the verses that you selected for your biblical basis of mission. For each verse ask three questions:

1. Does this verse give a command? What are we supposed to do? (Command)
2. Does this verse suggest a scope or extent? Who all is to be served? (Scope)
3. Does this verse suggest a result or benefit? What positive results should be expected? (Benefits)

Write out your answers in the work space below.

WORK SPACE:

Our Foundation for Mission Scriptures:

1. _____
2. _____
3. _____
4. _____
5. _____
6. _____

Commands	Scope	Benefits

Having answered these questions for each verse (note that not every verse answers all the questions), write a biblical mandate statement that says, basically, "We are commanded to *do what,* so that *who,* can *benefit how.*"

Here are some illustrations of what a team might write:

- The Scriptures require us to preach the gospel (Command) in all the world (Scope) so that everyone (Scope) has an opportunity to know Christ (Benefit).
- We are commanded to go to every nation, evangelizing and discipling people so that God may be glorified.
- The Bible tells us to reach all people groups, proclaiming the gospel, discipling believers and meeting human need so that people everywhere may be reconciled to God and to each other.

For an excellent study of the Great Commission passages, see *Commissioned* by Marvin Newell. (See **Resources**.)

WORK SPACE:

A Biblical Mandate Statement for our Mission Leadership Team (my draft):

_____

_____

_____

Biblical Mandate Statement for our Mission Leadership Team (team draft):

_____

_____

_____

_____

Scope

The scope or extent of ministry responsibility can be considered geographically, linguistically, or culturally. What groups are within our team's responsibility for ministry?

- People outside the U.S. only?
- People whose primary language is not English, whether in other countries or in our own?
- People who speak English but are culturally different from our church body, such as ethnic neighborhoods or inner city communities?
- People who are pretty much like us, such as our unchurched neighbors?

It may be useful to think of people in three categories:
- People unlike us far away
- People unlike us nearby
- People like us nearby

WORK SPACE:

Biblical Mandate Statement (with comments, suggestions, corrections from church leaders):

_____

_____

_____

Biblical Mandate Statement for our Mission Leadership Team (approved):

_____

_____

_____

Which of these categories belong to the mission team? Not infrequently, church leaders want the scope to be broader than the team would like. Church leaders may want to include all efforts outside the local body to be considered "mission." In one church, the mission team was asked to manage the church support for the denomination district office because this was money that "went out" from the church. The mission team often wants to limit their scope to people unlike us, people from other cultures, languages, and nations. The team may well argue that people like us are the responsibility of the local church leaders and congregation. They reason that the church body, as part of their Christian responsibility, should be reaching people where they live and work. Mission is going beyond this natural sphere of influence.

The scope issue must be acknowledged and worked out between church leaders and the team. Sometimes the issue is resolved by appointing two, or even three, separate teams, each with its own budget and area of responsibility. For example, a church might have one team for international ministries and another team for U.S. ministries. One church has a team for local same-culture ministries, a second for ministries to local internationals, and a third for global ministries. Another church has a global ministries team (that handles ministry among internationals whether outside or inside the U.S.), a local ministries team (that works with local community ministries such as Habitat for Humanity, Teen Challenge, a local foster parenting group, and a city literacy program) and a regional mission team (that works with the denomination district office and nearby church plants).

Stuff you need to know about Doing Missions in Your Church by David Mays (herein referred to as *Stuff*). Five volumes on one CD. Volume I, the Contents of all five volumes, and the Cumulative Index are available on the web for free. Purchase the CD from David Mays at www.davidmays.org.

"Missions Scope and Boundaries," *Stuff* vol. II, 11

"The Image and Substance of Missions," *Stuff* vol. V, 9

Authority

What is the team authorized to do without requesting permission? This is primarily a financial question. In general, church boards have full financial authority. A few churches have a mission board, separate from the church board, which has full authority to establish a budget and disburse funds. Committees and teams usually have an authorized spending limit. They are authorized to disburse funds according to an approved budget and may have authority to spend additional funds within a limit as long as the overall expenses are within budget. Beyond that, they operate in a "recommend" mode with approval being required from the church board. Committees and teams usually propose an annual budget and recommend additional or different expenditures as appropriate during the year.

Not infrequently the vision arising from the mission team may challenge the perspective of the church staff, elder board or finance committee, who may not have been focused on how much to trust the Lord for investment in mission. In such situations the mission team will prayerfully consider how to best present an expanded or ambitious new financial proposal. Vision can arise anywhere in the body. If God gives vision to the mission team, don't be surprised if the rest of the church leaders are not initially on the same wave length. Part of your responsibility as leaders is to encourage a God-sized vision for mission and the budget needed to support it.

WORK SPACE:

Scope

The scope of the Mission Leadership Team at our church includes:

Geographically: _____

Linguistically: _____

Culturally: _____

Authority

The Mission Leadership Team at our church has financial authority to

_____

_____

_____

FUNCTIONS
What are we supposed to do?

Communicate

With the current emphasis on mission trips, many people think trips are the primary team responsibility. One new mission team member said, "I thought that being on the mission team meant deciding where to take mission trips." Another man told his wife he was going to join the mission team. "Oh, where are you going?" she asked. It is true that mission trips take a great deal of planning and effort by mission teams, but trips are only one of several important responsibilities.

One of these is communication. An aim for any mission team is to make mission a normal, regular part of congregation life and ministry, not a once a year emphasis. Something that happens only once a year rarely changes someone's life pathway. The mission team wants to see every member regularly and routinely participating in mission in some way as a normal, organic part of the Christian life.

An aim for any mission team is to make mission a normal, regular part of congregation life.

To this end, the team wants to make mission both intensive and extensive. Intensive means a periodic intensive mission experience. Two generations ago, a week-long vacation Bible school or a summer youth camp often focused heavily on foreign mission.

Life-long commitments and life paths were forged during many of these experiences. A generation ago, God often interrupted people's lives during an eight-day mission conference or when they hosted a missionary family for several days. Today God grips people and changes their life trajectories more frequently at a college spiritual emphasis week, the Urbana Student Convention, or a mission trip. The team is responsible to provide such opportunities for youth and adults alike.

A few years ago, a new mission team chairman was asked to attend a national ACMC[1] Conference. During the three-days of Bible teaching and mission training, God overwhelmed his heart with the overarching imperative of reaching the world for Christ. Upon arrival back home, his wife asked him how it went. This calm, rational businessman burst into tears. His life trajectory had changed.

Make mission both intensive and extensive.

Extensive means that mission is everywhere present in the church. It is ubiquitous. You see it in the church buildings, in globes and banners, and displays and maps. You hear it in the message; you pray it in prayer; you sing it in worship; you hear it in reports; you study it in Scripture. Everywhere you look you see the evidence that this church is involved in God's mission in the world. It becomes part of your understanding of the Christian life.

Both intensive and extensive are necessary. People who grow up in a church that exhibits the Great Commission everywhere may understand it and agree to it but never commit their lives to it. Frequently God moves through an intensive experience to move people to life commitments. However, a life commitment based on an intensive experience may be short-lived without the reinforcement of ever-present, extensive mission.

WORK SPACE:

Mission is extensive in our church in the following ways. Here's how we see it communicated on a regular, ongoing basis:

_____

_____

_____

_____

_____

_____

_____

_____

Here are additional ways we could make mission extensive or ubiquitous in our church:

_____

_____

_____

_____

_____

These are the intensive mission experiences that occur related to our church:

_____

_____

Here are additional intensive mission experiences we could provide:

_____

_____

Our next steps are (person responsible, action step, date):

_____

_____

Education

Perhaps the most important element of communication is education. Of all the major elements of mission in a church, my experience suggests that education and discipleship are the most frequently neglected. Even churches that have a mission pastor and a well-functioning mission team rarely have an intentional, comprehensive and integrated process for educating and discipling the congregation in mission. Church leaders too often rely on an occasional message, video clip, financial appeal or mission event to generate resources for mission. If mission were only one of the *programs* of the church, this would be understandable and perhaps appropriate. Not everyone is expected to be knowledgeable about or involved in every church program. However, mission is part of the *purpose* of the church. Indeed, one could argue that mission—the discipling of all nations—is the *overarching* purpose. It is *the mission* of the church: thus it is for everyone. It is fundamental for all congregation members to learn, grow, commit, support, and become involved in mission for the church to maximize its effectiveness toward its purpose.

The mission team may be the first group needing education. Many people who join a mission team have a minimal understanding of what the Bible says about God's heart for the nations. They may have little idea of where Christian resources are plentiful or scarce in the world. They may have little background for evaluating the relative importance of various kinds of ministry. They may not be aware of the mission history of their own church. They don't know what mission work the church has undertaken in the past and what organizations and workers the church has supported and why. And they may not know whether those ministries have been effective. So the mission team must work to educate themselves and avoid the situation of the blind leading the blind.

Some areas for mission team education include Bible study on mission, mission history, biographies of great missionaries,

missionaries that represent your church, geography, cultures, mission organizations that work internationally, mission organizations that work in your city, mission strategies and where they apply, countries and ethnic groups, current world events and how they affect the life of believers and the spread of the gospel, American culture and how it affects our understanding of the Bible and Christian life, your church philosophy and policies, education tools available for the congregation, preparation required for short-term or long-term workers in other cultures, and mission resources.

The mission team may be looking for ways to help the church staff and board understand the overriding priority of the Great Commission.

What is true of the mission team is very likely also true of church leaders. Pastors may have taken only one introductory mission course in seminary and I've heard several say they didn't learn very much in that course. Lay leaders increasingly come from a non-religious background or a Christian experience where God's global purpose was not a significant factor. Thus, the mission team may be looking for ways to help the church staff and board or session understand the overriding priority of the Great Commission and what it means for your church.

In today's church the mission team seeks ways to supplement the limited mission education that comes from the pulpit. Pastors may have limited opportunities to preach on mission. On any given day, a significant portion of the congregation is absent. Presentations by long-term or short-term mission workers may be offered when most congregation members are not present. One Sunday a year devoted to global mission is woefully inadequate to generate understanding, let alone commitment, from most people. Jesus met with his disciples at least five times over six weeks after the resurrection to make sure the disciples grasped the Great Commission mandate. And that was after living with them day and night for three years. So we can't expect people to grasp it in a day or a weekend. Therefore, education and discipleship may depend on the mission team. Finding effective ways to help educate the congregation is perhaps one of the biggest challenges.

"Five Elements of Missions Education," www.DavidMays.org/elements.html

"Four Kinds of Pastors," www.DavidMays.org/pastors.html

Awareness

Communication, however, is more than education, although education is perhaps the most frequently missing piece. The mission team has the responsibility to stimulate mission awareness. Mission awareness implies knowledge of current happenings, of what is going on. One area is world events, particularly in regard to Christianity or other religions. Where is God obviously at work? Where is Christianity advancing? Where is there religious conflict? Where are Christians being persecuted? Where have governments, wars, or natural disasters made people vulnerable? What are the needs? Who is helping? Where have such events created openness to the Gospel? What mission groups are working there? How can we pray? What kinds of stories are coming back about what God is doing?

Another area of awareness is what is happening in our city or community. What are the major demographic groups? What changes are occurring? What ministries are operating and what are they doing? Who from our church is involved? Do we have a church partnership in this area? What are they learning? Who else can help? What do they need?

A third area of awareness is what our long-term missionaries and partners are doing overseas. What is their vision? What are their goals? What is God accomplishing through them? What are their current circumstances? What are their needs? How else can we help? What about people from our church who are going or have returned from their location? What did they face? What did they learn? Whom did they serve and what were those people like? What did they need? Where did they see God at work?

WORK SPACE:

These are subject areas that have been included in education opportunities in our church during the past year:

_____

_____

_____

_____

Here are some subject areas we might include in the future:

_____

_____

_____

_____

These departments, ministries, or groups, included some form of mission education in their ministry during the past six months:

_____

_____

_____

_____

We want to approach these departments, ministries, or groups in the next six months about including mission education in their ministry:

_____

_____

_____

_____

The following opportunities for mission awareness have been provided to our church in the past six months:

_____

_____

_____

_____

The following are possible opportunities we suggest for our church in the next six months:

_____

_____

_____

_____

Our next team steps in regard to education opportunities for our church are (person responsible, action steps, date):

_____

_____

_____

_____

Promotion

The mission team is also in the promotion business. Promotion basically means publicity, advertising, attracting (positive) attention. The team is responsible to be sure that people know that the church is involved in mission and it pertains to them, to alert the congregation to mission activities and events, and to stimulate their response to needs and opportunities. Needs might include things like issues for prayer, logistics for a city project, help preparing for an upcoming mission event, or providing supplies or assistance to a missionary or worker. Opportunities might include upcoming trips, a forthcoming mission course, a mission emphasis weekend, serving in some capacity on the mission team, or teaching or facilitating a mission class.

Promotion may include clever pulpit announcements, mailings, attractive literature, well-done video, web pages, culturally sensitive appeals, and personal persuasion. People think things are important if they look important, so promotion must be done with excellence. Further, people are subconsciously influenced by who does the promoting, how voluminous and multi-faceted it is, and how long in advance something is advertised.

People think things are important
if they look important.

Prayer

The team also carries a responsibility to ensure that people pray for the world, for the lost and hurting, for mission work, for countries and nations, for persecuted believers, for leaders and workers in the community and around the world, for the church in mission and for their own commitment and involvement. The team can make available prayer tools, schedule special prayer events, ensure that prayer for mission is included in regular corporate prayer and other prayer initiatives, and help leaders include it as a regular part of all church ministries and programs. And, of course, the mission team should be the leaders in praying.

Global Day of Prayer, www.globaldayofprayer.com

Global Prayer Digest, www.globalprayerdigest.org

International Day of Prayer for the Persecuted Church, www.persecutedchurch.org

Muslim Prayer Focus, 30-Days of Prayer for the Muslim World during Ramadan, www.30-days.net

Operation World Prayer Guide, www.operationworld.org

Praying Through the 10/40 Window, www.win1040.com

Stewardship

Often the mission team carries some responsibility for mission stewardship of the congregation. This, of course, must be coordinated with church leaders, but church leaders often welcome the insights and assistance of the mission team for encouraging liberal giving of the congregation for mission.

Mission Events

Communication responsibilities are often connected to annual (or semi-annual or quarterly) mission emphasis events in the church. Because such events have sometimes become ho-hum for congregation members, it is important that seminars, conferences, and activities be planned with a variety of backgrounds and age groups in mind and that they be promoted with excellence and passion by all church leaders. Church leaders must participate and appear in a leadership role, even if all the work has been done by the team. The event must fit the culture of the church and live up to its billing in quality.

"Missions Conference Evaluation for Church Leaders," *Stuff* vol. III, 30

"Missions Conference Evaluation for the Congregation," *Stuff* vol. II, 28

WORK SPACE:

The following mission prayer tools, opportunities, and encouragements have been provided to our congregation in the past six months:

_____

_____

We plan to provide the following prayer tools, opportunities, and encouragements to our congregation – or to specific departments, ministries or groups – in the next six months (persons responsible, actions steps, and date):

_____

_____

_____

Our last mission event was held on _____

The objectives were:

The primary activities were:

On a scale of 1 (poor) to 5 (excellent), I rate the success of the event at: ___
For the next mission event, I suggest (date, purpose, theme, activities):

_____

_____

_____

_____

Our next steps in regard to a mission event are (person responsible, action steps, date):

_____

_____

_____

_____

Plan

Priorities and Goals

The needs for mission work are endless whereas resources are limited. Church leaders must exercise priorities. Financial and involvement decisions are made on the basis of some things being more important than others. The priorities may be well thought out and consistent or they may be pragmatic and change frequently. It may be worthwhile to identify and state the priorities that drive decisions and examine their appropriateness.

Who benefits most from the identified priorities? Are these the best priorities? Financial support decisions can be made for a variety of reasons, some better than others, some perhaps hidden. For example:

- This is the most effective way to help fulfill the Great Commission.
- This best fits the interests and gifting of our congregation.
- This provides help for people we know and love who feel called to ministry.
- This supports organizations or ministries that are championed by some of our people.
- This builds a relationship with people we consider important and want to befriend.
- This fulfills an obligation to a former seminary colleague, relative or friend.

Three foundations for priorities might be:

1. What does Scripture require?
2. What helps us make the biggest possible impact on the world for Christ?
3. For what kinds of ministry roles has God best equipped our church?

The mission team has the responsibility to recommend, and sometimes to decide, priorities and goals for the church's mission efforts. This means interpreting from Scripture what ministries are most critical. It means learning about the various countries and peoples of the world: what needs are most urgent, what needs are not being met, what peoples are being neglected, what organizations and churches are working in those areas. It means considering what kinds of ministries, locations, partners, and workers are most appropriate for your church. This obviously implies considerable research to understand the Scripture, the world, your church and these times. It is important to understand your church and your congregation. What ministries and workers have been wholeheartedly supported by the congregation? What kinds of roles fit the gifting and personality of your congregation? What ministries are championed by Godly, enthusiastic, well-grounded, reliable leaders or congregation members?

The alternative to understanding Scripture, the world, and your church, is to respond to the visions and passions of others, perhaps the most aggressive outside solicitor, the ministry that a church leader favors, or the most pressing nearby need.

The team will recommend, for example, what proportion of efforts are dedicated to people of other countries or cultures vs. people of your own country, city, or culture, how much to evangelistic and discipleship ministries vs. humanitarian (compassion, justice, and poverty) issues, how much to the support of individual workers vs. the support of partner organizations, how much to the support of your own denomination or your favorite mission organizations vs. other organizations, and how much to ministries you feel are most critical vs. other ministries your church has been supporting or considering.

It is my contention that the imperatives of Scripture and the needs of the world should be the primary shapers of a church's mission work. The best plan is for a church to identify and undertake—or at least include—the most crucial work needed for expanding the Kingdom and reaching the least served. However, an alternative church philosophy that has merit is to pursue the mission work championed by individual enthusiasts in the church. When congregation members have a burning issue, fan it into flame. Empower these individuals to champion their causes, to inform, inspire, recruit, and develop teams to undertake mission work. Encourage and support these teams. Incorporate them as full partners in the mission ministry. Internal champions can multiply the number of people in ministry. It is much easier to support people in their ministry than to recruit them to your ministry.

> *The imperatives of Scripture and the needs of the world should be the primary shapers of a church's mission work.*

The philosophy and mode of operation of church leaders often tips the scales on how the mission team establishes priorities. If the church operates primarily by responding to the senior pastor's vision, then the mission team will most effectively operate by supporting the senior pastor's vision. If the church operates largely by departments and ministries setting direction, the mission team will best operate in this manner. If programs and activities are initiated and shaped by enthusiastic champions who initiate ministries and assemble a team around them, then this may be the best method of operation for the mission team. Such bottom-up leadership can greatly expand the capacity of the church's involvement in mission.

It is valuable for the mission team to write out their priorities and formulate them into specific faith goals.

Building Global Vision by David Mays
"Developing a Missions Strategy that Fits Your Church," free on the web or purchase on CD, www.davidmays.org

Priority Questions for the Mission Ministry

Audience
How important is it to work toward reaching or ministering to particular groups of people? This may be indicated by continents, countries, religious groups, or people groups.

Balance
How important is it to achieve a better balance of local and global efforts? Do we need to adjust the distribution of our budget dollars, workers, projects, or partnerships?

Focus
Should we shine a beacon or glow with 1000 points of light? How important is it to adjust our focus? Is it better to do one big thing, many small things, or somewhere in between?

History
How much should we continue the mission efforts and values of the past? How much do we need to change and how quickly?

'Our Own'
How important is it to support those we already know or who are part of our congregation or fellowship? How willing are we to partner with others?

Our Roles
How important is it to engage in ministry that fits the gifts, skills, vocations, and inclinations of our congregation?

Participation
How important is it that our people be able to contribute hands-on to the ministry? How important is it that we work in areas that are safe, close, or cost effective for our travel?

Partnership
How important is it that our congregation partner with other entities in mission work? How important is it that the projects or missionaries we support are part of larger partnership efforts?

Task
How important is it for us to evaluate, select, and support more strategic, critical, and urgent ministry tasks? How important is it to avoid or minimize less strategic ministry opportunities?

WORK SPACE:

The most important priorities for our church mission ministry should be:

_____

_____

_____

_____

_____

Our church could achieve better balance in ministry by:

_____

_____

_____

_____

_____

The most important tasks for our mission ministry are:

_____

_____

_____

_____

The most important geographic areas, countries, languages, cultures, religions, and/or people groups for us to serve are:

_____

_____

_____

Our most effective roles in mission as a church are:

_____

_____

_____

_____

Strategy

A strategy is a roadmap. It is a statement of how you intend to deploy your resources to attain your goals or focus on your priorities. Every church has a strategy in some form. It may be a written strategy with clear goals that is faithfully followed. Or it may exist only in the minds of key decision makers. In any case there are reasons and values behind the decisions that are made to invest mission resources. *Someone* has a strategy. One or more people in the church often take the lead in deciding where mission resources go. It may be a pastor, a mission enthusiast, the elder board, the denomination, parents of missionaries, or someone in leadership with a strong voice. The values behind those decisions may be commonly known and shared, or they may be unknown (under the table) or not understood. Every mission organization has a strategy to recommend for your church. Frequently church strategies are composed of a mosaic of the visions and strategies of various mission organizations, missionaries, and church leaders. Obviously, not all church mission strategies are equally strategic.

A strategy is a statement of how you intend to deploy your resources to attain your goals.

An important part of developing a mission strategy is to clarify how mission decisions have been made in the past and how they are being made now. What are the *values* and *priorities* that drive the decisions? It is important that the decision-making group clarify, openly and honestly, why they make the decisions they do and why their predecessors made the decisions they did. Do we follow historical precedent? Do we favor people we know or those a key person knows? Does the team vote the party line with our denomination? Do some have vested interests in particular missionaries or organizations? Do team members tend to submit to an individual they respect? Are team members intimidated by a strong personality? Do they accept a proposal because they want to be team players and it is uncomfortable to disagree? In order to agree on a direction, team members need to be clear and open about their motives and submit these motives and priorities prayerfully to God for his direction.

A good strategy is based on objective facts, well-reasoned priorities, open and honest discussion, deep prayer, and full commitment. It provides an overall plan to pursue important ministries where they are most needed by the best methods that call on the talents, gifting, and inclinations of the congregation. You might decide to develop two strategies, one for *deploying* your church's resources (external) and one for *mobilizing* your church's resources (internal).

"Template for a Missions Strategy," *Stuff* vol. IV, 35

"Developing a Missions Strategy that Fits Your Church," free on the web or purchase on CD, www.davidmays.org

One-Year and Five-Year Objectives and Budgets

The final portion of a strategy is a set of targets. Objectives are what you hope and plan to accomplish in a given time frame. In the best case they include statements of desired field results supported by investment targets.

Projected investments are easily expressed in terms of budget categories. A budget category or "bucket" is named for the goal or priority. Current dollars, percentage of the budget, partners, and/ or numbers of workers deployed toward this goal or priority area is listed on one line, and the resources you intend to deploy in the next year and in following years are put on subsequent lines.

"Developing a Missions Strategy that Fits Your Church,"
www.davidmays.org

"Resource Distribution Grids for Missions Prioritizing, Planning,
and Decision Making," www.DavidMays.org/grids.html

"Examples of Church Missions Funding Strategies,"
www.DavidMays.org/fund.html

"What is the Best Way to Fund Missions in Our Church?"
www.davidmays.org/funding2.pdf

"What Belongs in the Missions Budget?" www.davidmays.org/
Budget.pdf

WORK SPACE:
Analyze your current mission budget and your priorities. Complete one of the
two budget grids below, or modify one of them to suit your needs and fill it out.

Deployment of Mission Resources	Internal	Local	Global		
	Trips* Education	Projects Partnerships	General	Specific Project	Unreached People
NOW					
% of mission dollars					
# of full-time missionaries					
# of short-term workers					
# of partnerships					
GOAL – Next Year					
% of mission dollars					
# of full-time missionaries					
# of short-term workers					
# of partnerships					
GOAL – 3 Years					
% of mission dollars					
# of full-time missionaries					
# of short-term workers					
# of partnerships					

Deployment of Mission Resources	Internal	Local	Local	International	
	Trips* Education	Evangelistic	Compassion	General	Unreached
NOW					
% of mission dollars					
# of full-time workers					
# of short-term workers					
Strength of partnerships (1 to 5)					
GOAL – 3 YEARS					
% of mission dollars					
# of missionaries					
# of short-term workers					
Strength of partnerships (1 to 5)					

*In the above examples, mission trips are located in the internal section of the budget because most mission trips are more accurately classified as vision, discipleship, or exploration trips. The primary objectives and results of most trips relate to the growth of the person who goes and the benefit to the sending church. Thus they should be considered an educational or overhead cost rather than a ministry investment. Alternatives are to fund mission trips from other departments depending on who is sponsoring or going on the trip (for example, youth), or to fund mission trips outside the budget through special support or other fund raising.

   "Mission Trip Funding Options," *Stuff* vol. II, 55

Manage
The Team

All functioning teams require a certain amount of administrative work, mission teams more than some. The team has to decide when and how often they will meet, who chairs the meetings, who keeps the records, how many members to have, how they are to be selected, how long they will serve, how decisions will be made, and so forth. They have to agree on their responsibilities and figure out how they will divide the work, set objectives, and hold themselves accountable for completing them. In today's world, they will often minimize the number of group meetings and use alternative means to communicate and keep track of progress through email, phone calls, and subgroup meetings.

Policies and Procedures

These functional procedures are often included as one part of a mission policy or a mission policies and procedures manual. Many churches have developed extensive manuals but follow them sporadically. Other churches prefer to operate more informally because a policy feels too restrictive. The downside of freewheeling is that decisions may be arbitrary or whimsical, and consistency depends on the longevity and continuity of a mission team.

However sketchy or detailed your policies, it may be wise to identify and write out your core values, the most important principles by which you intend to operate. Committing to and operating on the basis of agreed upon values provides flexibility and accommodates spontaneity without sacrificing consistency and direction. Following are some sample mission values (abbreviated) taken from actual church mission documents. Note that these are a mixture of operational values and ministry values or priorities. The latter should be consistent with your ministry priorities and goals.

Mission Values from Local Churches

Alignment with our church statement of faith

Church-wide involvement

Community transformation

Complete accountability and transparency.

Demonstrate respect for the differences and dignity of others.

Directed by the Holy Spirit

Empowering and equipping our church

Equipping nationals

Excellence in stewardship of our resources

Hearing and obeying God

Honesty, integrity and trustworthiness in all of our activities.

Indigenous ministry

Ministries that support both physical and spiritual needs

Mobilization of people for mission

Opportunities for multiplication

Partnering with like-minded mission agencies and churches

Personal & active roles for our congregation

Personal relationships with our global partners

Planting of churches where Christ is not known.

Sending church: We should be a developing and supporting church.

Strategic ministry and long-term partnerships

The unreached

Transformation

Unreached people group focus

A primary part of a policy manual is the financial section. Church leaders often want to systematize the criteria for deciding on a partner, what qualifies an organization or individual for financial support, when support begins and ends, how much support to provide, what disqualifies a person or organization for further support, what evaluation is to be done before and throughout a partnership, what is provided for retirement of a worker, how much of the finances are to be used for internal expenses, and many other things.

"Benefits of a Missions Policy," *Stuff* vol. I, 40

"Steps for Developing a Missions Policy," *Stuff* vol. I, 41

"Developing or Revising Your Missions Policy," *Stuff* vol. III, 7

The *Church Missions Policy Handbook* by ACMC provides guidance for sections on Purpose, Structure, Responsibilities and Finances. Twenty seven different issues are listed for financial policies.

WORK SPACE:

Our Core Values for Operation are:

_____

_____

_____

We have a mission policy.

___Yes ___ No ___ I think so. ___ I don't know.

We use it

___ Frequently, ___ Occasionally, ___ Rarely, ___ We can't find it.

___ It works well. ___ It is out of date in a few areas.

___ It is out of date in many areas. ___ It no longer works for us.

We need a good policy. ___ Yes ___ No ___ It doesn't matter.

It should be ___ longer and more detailed than our current one,

___ shorter and easier to use.

We need it primarily for:

_____

_____

We will undertake to write or update our mission policy. ___ Yes ___ No

The best person to write the first draft is: _____

Our next step is (person responsible, action step, date):

_____

Resources

When we speak of resources for mission, we usually think of money, workers and prayer. However, churches are blessed with a huge variety of resources, many of which can be highly productive for mission if employed in the right situations. Consider an exercise in which your team identifies as many resources as you can think of that are available, or potentially available, to your congregation. Put these resources or assets in two categories: fixed and portable. Fixed assets include your church facility and most of your people. Portable assets include your dollars, a few of your people, and many other things. Include skills (and talents and gifts), experiences, relationships, and influence. Consider access to information, government officials, products available to employees, international connections, and so forth. When workshop participants engage in this exercise, the resulting array of resources is astounding.

Use fixed resources locally and portable resources globally.

As you list resources as fixed or portable, be aware that fixed assets can only be employed where they are. Portable resources can be employed anywhere. Therefore, to maximize your use of resources, follow this principle: As much as possible use your fixed assets locally and use your portable assets globally. One practical example of this is to deploy volunteers into local mission efforts where possible rather than to financially support paid workers for the same work. Remember this list of resources (and add to it) when you are considering how to support your workers and missionaries and help them be more effective in ministry.

WORK SPACE:

Resources available to our congregation:

Portable Resources: Fixed Resources:

_____   _____

_____   _____

_____   _____

_____   _____

_____   _____

_____   _____

Mission Budget

Establishing a budget for the coming year comes naturally as part of the goal-setting process. Proposing a budget is much simpler when you can extrapolate from the past year's budget, making adjustments for ministries, projects, or partnerships that you want to cap or reduce and making increases for ministries, projects, partnerships, or workers that you believe deserve more effort or new effort. Anticipating the addition of new projects or workers helps establish the baseline for the coming year. Requests for additional funding are greatly strengthened when you show specific, worthy goals that your team feels strongly your church should pursue.

Requests for additional funding are greatly strengthened when you show specific, worthy goals that your church should pursue.

If your team is responsible for both local and international ministry, the budget may be set up with a category for each. You may want a separate category for any particular area or focus that you want to increase (or decrease). For example, if your team wants to increase your focused efforts toward reaching a particular unreached group or to extend more efforts for the unreached in general, you may set up a budget category for this focus. The team may want a separate budget category for overseas mission trips, or any other type of activity that requires a significant portion of the budget that you want to monitor, limit, or increase. The budget will include a category for internal expenses such as discipleship materials, educational conferences and seminars, printing or video preparation of promotional materials, the mission emphasis event, special speakers, mission trips, and perhaps your team's support of mission efforts undertaken by other church departments such as helping the youth with their mission trips.

Of course, the team must administer the mission budget. Much of this is routine, requesting the church treasurer to send checks on a regular basis to approved partners, workers, organizations and projects. However, there are always many items that are not routine. These may include handling donations and expenditures for mission trips and projects jointly sponsored by more than one department, such as youth mission projects. Any special needs or requests must be considered and, if approved, the finances must be handled appropriately.

Church Missions Policy Handbook, ACMC

"What Belongs in the Missions Budget?" www.DavidMays.org/Budget.pdf

---

WORK SPACE:

In our church the mission budget is

put together by _____,

discussed by _____,

and approved by _____.

The following elements provide input for a new mission budget for our church (ranked from most important to least important):

___ what we did last year

___ requests that come from our missionaries, partners and outside organizations

___ recommendations from church leaders

___ our mission goals for the coming year

___ other _____

WORK SPACE:

The following steps would help our team produce a more effective budget:

_____

_____

_____

_____

_____

Our team will take the following steps to put together next year's budget (person responsible, action step, date):

_____

_____

_____

_____

Evaluate

Periodically the team will review all aspects of the mission ministry, both internal operations and deployment of resources. Evaluating mission results is a little like evaluating research. The scientist can't control, and often can't predict, the outcomes. Judgment is based on how someone plans, works the plan, exercises diligence, evaluates interim outcomes, and adjusts to the unexpected. In other words, it's not straightforward.

Considering how resources are invested is one way to evaluate. How much are you putting into mission? How many workers, how many dollars, how much volunteer effort, and how much prayer did your church provide? These are very important because they limit what we can expect. But it is also important to evaluate whether those resources were invested in the right priorities, people, partnerships, and projects.

Another approach is to ask how well the church is operating in mission. The team may formulate and ask questions about topics such as:

- Church leader involvement
- Congregational awareness and commitment
- The planning process
- Mission strategy
- How well the mission work aligns with the church's philosophy and values
- How well the team operates and cooperates
- How well mission is integrated throughout the departments and age groups of the congregation
- Personal involvement of congregation members
- Corporate encouragement of mission giving
- Proportion of church finances committed to mission
- How well leaders are recruiting and preparing workers
- Effectiveness of mission publicity
- Congregational prayer for the world, the lost, the hurting and your workers and partners
- How well the church cares for and supports workers in difficult places
- Relevance and effectiveness of the mission ministry in today's culture

Perhaps the best tool available is the Missions Assessment Profile (MAP) from ACMC.

The Missions Assessment Profile, ACMC
"Evaluating Missions in the Local Church," *Stuff* vol. 1, 45
"Global Ministry Self Assessment," *Stuff* vol. III, 22
"Missions Assessment Profile," *Stuff* vol. IV, 13

Ten Questions Every Church Should Ask About Their Mission Ministry

Leadership Involvement. Do the pastor, staff, elders, and other church leaders take the lead through direction setting, personal involvement, and enthusiasm?

Heart. Is the congregation winning people to Christ at home and serving in their community consistent with their desire for missionaries to win people to Christ elsewhere and help those in need?

Planning. Does the church set goals, carry them out and evaluate progress for internal mobilization and external deployment of missionaries?

Strategy. Does the church have a direction or focus for its mission work?

Congruence. Does the church support mission work consistent with the values and philosophy of the church's own work?

Mission Leadership Team. Is the mission leadership team organized and effective?

Integration. Does mission permeate the age groups, interest levels, programs, and calendar of the church?

Congregation Participation. Does a large portion of the congregation participate regularly by giving, praying, serving, teaching, and/or ministering?

Finances. Is church funding for mission a large percentage of the church budget, provided for by a large percentage of the congregation well representing all adult age categories?

Relevance. Is the church in touch with modern realities with regard to its mission work, mission image, communication methods, partnering and networking?

WORK SPACE:

Consider the ten questions every church should ask.

Our church is strongest in the following areas:

_____

_____

_____

Our church could improve the most in mission by working in the following area(s):

_____

_____

_____

Our team will begin work in these areas:

_____

_____

_____

Our first steps (person responsible, action step, date):

Area: _____

Person: _____

Step: _____ Date: _____

Area: _____

Person: _____

Step: _____ Date: _____

Area: _____

Person: _____

Step: _____ Date: _____

Mobilize

Mobilization refers to the entire process of marshalling resources for deployment. The mission team is a mobilization unit, each member a mobilizer. "A mobilizer is a normal, everyday Christian who walks with God, yet has a global perspective and stays on the home front to rouse others to action."[2] The goal is to help people along a journey, a lifestyle of being engaged with God on mission to the nations.

Discipling and Equipping

Beyond educating the church leaders and congregation in mission, the mission team has the responsibility to disciple people in God's global mission. It means to help them learn, grow, pray, give, serve, and go. It includes education but it is more personal, focused, and spiritually oriented than education. It means helping people to commit to Christ and his mission, to grow in their understanding, to find their roles, and to begin and sustain a lifetime of involvement. Discipleship is a heavy responsibility, especially considering that many congregation members exhibit less than full commitment to Christ and may be in church only two or three times a month. The motivation for growth and commitment arises from a deep understanding of God's grace in one's own life, discovering the pervasive theme of God's heart for all nations in the Scripture, experiencing people with great needs, and recognizing that one can have an important and fruitful role. Creativity, diligence, and the help of church leaders and volunteers may be necessary.

One avenue for developing discipleship opportunities for people in your church is to work with existing groups and ministries to incorporate mission Bible study, education, prayer, and experience into their regular patterns. This means finding and building trust relationships with leaders and offering your assistance. Most churches have few leaders and many followers, but personal and small group mentoring is still important for discipling.

Evangelism Training

Christians often feel inadequate to explain the gospel and are concerned about offending people because of our cultural commitment to tolerance. As Todd Ahrend says, "More and more commonly in the United States, you are viewed as backward, ignorant, extremely arrogant, and shallow if you hold that Christ is the only way."[3] While service projects and partnerships provide opportunity to get to know people in need, few people come to Christ without hearing the Gospel message. Learning to share your testimony and explain the Gospel is, perhaps, a neglected area of training in many churches today.

Service Projects

A number of churches are urging their congregations to get involved in service projects in their communities. In some cases a church pastor or the mission team develops a partnership with a local ministry and then arranges for teams from the church to travel together on certain days to volunteer with the ministry. In other cases, existing small groups are encouraged to find needs in their community and work together to meet those needs. In most cases the training is hands-on. Get involved and learn as you go. A number of churches have found that people come to their church *because* of their community service ministries. Some of these people are not yet believers but they want to help others. The service ministries serve as evangelism opportunities for these people. As they get involved in ministry to others, side-by-side with believers, they are influenced for Christ.

WORK SPACE:

These are the ways education and discipleship are being carried out in our congregation:

_____

_____

_____

These are the ways evangelism training is being carried out:

_____

_____

_____

These are the service projects being planned or carried out:

_____

_____

_____

_____

Our team is working with the following leaders, ministries, and groups to help them incorporate mission projects into their ministries:

_____

_____

_____

These team members will approach the following leaders to help them incorporate one of the above:

Team Member	Ministry Leader
_____	_____
_____	_____
_____	_____

Mission Trips

Mission trips have become a major part of many church mission ministries. Almost all long-term overseas workers under 60 years of age have experienced a mission trip. Many people who support mission, pray for the lost and missionaries, and give substantially for mission were awakened to the importance of mission on a mission trip. At the same time, many mission trips produce very limited benefits. Many factors work together to make trips productive on the field, fruitful in the life of the people who go, and stimulating to the congregation that sent them. These include carefully selecting your partner on the field, going where you are wanted and needed, providing what is requested, sending the right people, being spiritually prepared, developing good teamwork, learning about the people in advance, being culturally sensitive, going as learners, and so forth.

"Standards of Excellence in Short-Term Missions," www. stmstandards.org,

Serving with Eyes Wide Open, David Livermore

Trip Stuff, 230 documents mostly developed by local churches (on CD) by David Mays. Purchase from David Mays. See www. davidmays.org/Resources/trip.html

Follow up

Perhaps the most neglected part of mission trips and projects is the follow through. What happens after the trip or the project? One day in the city or two weeks in another country can have a powerful impact on a person's life trajectory. But it can also quickly fade to a fond or troubling memory under the press of daily life. Often a huge investment is made in the mission trip. The mission team has the opportunity to build on that investment. Perhaps one goal for every mission trip is for everyone who goes to grow into a lifetime commitment to mission that is worked out through prayer and giving and, perhaps, long-term mission involvement. Confront each participant with the self-diagnostic question, "How will this short-term mission trip alter my long-term vision for my life?" [4]

Perhaps the most neglected part of mission trips and projects is the follow through.

The team can devise ways to build on the dramatic impact of the trip. These might include debriefing sessions after the trip to help all individuals consolidate and express what they learned, opportunities to describe their experience to church groups, periodic reunions of those who went, an ongoing class on mission, or placement in a community ministry.

WORK SPACE:

Following are the ministries and groups and their service projects and mission trips conducted or planned for the next six months:

Ministry/Group	Project or Trip
_____	_____
_____	_____
_____	_____
_____	_____

These are the strong points of the service projects and mission trips conducted so far:

_____

_____

_____

_____

_____

One good approach is to assign a mission-experienced mentor to each individual who returns from a trip. Returnees meet with their mentors periodically over the coming year to process what God is teaching them and the steps they are taking to live it out. People are often tired and overwhelmed after a trip, making follow up difficult. It is therefore important to make the follow through a part of the trip expectations from the beginning of planning.

"Mission Trip Follow Through," *Stuff* vol. II, 58
Trip Stuff, by David Mays

We are Strong (S) or Weak (W) in

_____ advance preparation

_____ developing advance relationships on the field

_____ providing what the field needs

_____ preparing the team in language and culture

_____ building teamwork

_____ leading the team

_____ serving with gladness on the field

_____ debriefing those who went

_____ following through with those who went

Our mission trips could be most helped by strengthening the areas of:

_____

_____

_____

We will contact and seek to help the following leaders, ministries, and groups to incorporate service projects or mission trips into their ministries:

_____

_____

Partner

The day of the lone ranger is past except for a few very specialized tasks and some very remote locations. Even those doing translation work among isolated tribes benefit immensely by constant communication with other linguists and translators. Everyone is working in partnership these days. However, partnering means many different things to different people, groups, and cultures. In Africa, a partnership might imply a blood-brother bond that lasts beyond death and includes mutual sharing of resources for extended family needs. At the other extreme, partnership might be just another name for financially supporting a missionary. According to Daniel Rickett, "a partnership is a complementary relationship driven by a common purpose and sustained by a willingness to learn and grow together in obedience to God."[5]

"All effective partnering initiatives are driven by an energizing, challenging vision. This vision must be a God-sized vision – beyond the capacity of any single person or agency to achieve alone. It must also be a God-glorifying vision – a ministry goal that clearly advances God's kingdom."[6]

Partner Criteria

The mission team will evaluate potential partners for ministry. With whom do you want to work? How do you decide? Perhaps your church has been closely connected to a mission organization for a long time—perhaps your denomination sending board or a particular mission agency—and you value that relationship. You know how to work together. You have confidence in their vision, leadership, and methods of operation. You want to continue to work together wherever possible. Perhaps you have been supporting a worker or a mission organization in a passive way but now you want to become more proactive, taking more ownership, perhaps helping investigate new initiatives or deploying more people into the work.

Maybe you are considering beginning work in a new area, such as a new kind of ministry, or an unreached people group, or a location in your city. How do you evaluate potential partners?

Of course you want to consider their doctrinal statement. Do you agree on the fundamentals? And do you resonate with their purpose, vision and goals? Do they place a high value on reaching people for Jesus? Do they have dynamic leadership? Do they exhibit financial responsibility? Do they have a track record? Are they effective in ministry? Are they serious about partnering with you as opposed to simply wanting financial support? Do they provide good training? If you are sending workers outside the country, do they have good member care? Do you fit relationally? Is there an obvious connection with, or the likelihood of good connections, with your church? Is there a strong sense of team?

"Agency Partnerships – Criteria for Assessment and Review," *Stuff* vol. III, 27

"Church-Agency Partnership Agreement," *Stuff* vol. II, 37

Potential Partners

National workers

National churches

National church denominations

National Christian mission organizations

National NGOs

Denomination sending board

US based independent mission agencies

US based NGOs

Other local North American churches

Local Christian ministry organizations

US campus ministries

Local secular and government organizations

Combinations of the above

Facilitating Partnerships

Partnerships are like marriages. They don't just happen and friction is inevitable. You have to work at it. A partnership will require someone from your church that has primary responsibility for developing the partnership, preparing appropriate agreements, facilitating ongoing partnering, and helping resolve conflict. If you are partnering with a national church or organization in another culture, much more preparation and maintenance will be needed. You need someone in the ministry location that understands both cultures and can serve as a go-between.

Building Strategic Relationships and *Making Your Partnership Work* by Daniel Rickett
"Global Partnering Growing Pains," four articles by Ellen Livingood,
www.catalystservices.org/bm~doc/ptshp-chal-i.pdf
www.catalystservices.org/bm~doc/ptshp-chal-ii.pdf
www.catalystservices.org/bm~doc/ptshp-chal-iii.pdf
www.catalystservices.org/bm~doc/clarify-expectations.pdf

WORK SPACE:

Our current mission ministry partners are (partner, field of ministry, ministry task, facilitator):

_____

_____

The partnerships that are working the best are _____

_____

_____

because _____

The partnership(s) that need the most attention are _____

_____

_____

because _____

Send

Mission trips have already been discussed. Here we look at vocational missionaries and longer-term workers. It is increasingly common to hear believers who purposefully represent Christ in their homes, businesses, schools, or communities referred to as missionaries. Such people are also properly called Christians, disciples, or followers of Jesus. It is helpful to maintain a distinctive meaning for the word "missionary." Christians, even devoted followers, are not all missionaries in a more narrow sense of the term.

Not all people concerned with health care are called medical doctors. And calling them all doctors would not help us communicate better. Missionaries, usually through considerable experience and/or training, learn to observe, listen, understand, live, model, communicate, provide assistance, share the gospel, and do various kinds of ministry among cultures and languages and in places that

The steps we will take with these partners are _____

_____

_____

We would like to find partners for

_____

_____

_____

Our team will take the following steps (person responsible, action step, date):

_____

_____

_____

_____

are not native to them. And they cross those barriers for extended periods of time for the sake of Christ and the gospel. Missionaries are "sent" as ambassadors to do the work of God where most of us cannot go and stay long enough to become effective.

A missionary works vocationally among people unlike himself for the sake of the Gospel.

Thus, a missionary is a God-appointed servant who is prepared and sent across boundaries and barriers to do God's work in another country, language, and/or culture for an extended period of time. Or, more succinctly, a missionary works vocationally among people unlike himself for the sake of the Gospel.

One important reason for this distinction is that a great number of people in the world will only receive life in Jesus if Christian workers cross geographic and cultural barriers, learn the language and the customs, live among the people, learn to understand and love them, help them to discover life in Christ, teach them the Scriptures, and show them how to live the Christian life. In other words, long-term missionaries are still needed.

Some missionaries go on their own. They set their own direction, chart their own course, and sometimes pay their own way. Most, however, need financial support from back home. Some churches send missionaries without utilizing a mission organization and attempt to provide shepherding, strategizing, supervising, and support systems. As Bill Taylor has said, however, few churches can really do all these things well.[7] For most churches the best route is to work in partnership with a mission sending agency.

In addition to sending missionaries, the church may also send vocational workers to do mission in their own cities and communities. As our world becomes more interconnected and culturally, linguistically, and religiously mixed, the distinction between "missionaries" and other Christian workers begins to break down. Many workers in our own cities must learn cross-cultural skills and develop new thinking patterns and learn to love people quite unlike themselves to be effective, in other words, they must become missionaries.

Further, ordinary Christians now have to cross the very significant barriers of worldview and differing understandings of the same language to communicate with near neighbors. We now have multiplied opportunities to learn, practice, and exercise cross-cultural skills in our neighborhoods and workplaces.

Throughout this book I use the word "worker" to include all vocational workers in their home cultures as well as short-termers at home or abroad, in their own culture or another culture. I use the word "missionary" to refer specifically to vocational workers crossing boundaries of culture, language, and/or distance for purposes of mission.

> *The most likely sources of potential*
> *workers in your church are students*
> *and mission trip alumni.*

Recruiting and Training

The most likely sources of potential workers in your church are students and mission trip alumni. Perhaps the mission team will make it a matter of regular prayer that God will alert church pastors, elders, and members of the mission team to those individuals who have a special devotion to God and who exhibit particular skills that God can use in full-time mission, especially an aptitude for cross-cultural relationships. Is God raising up young people in your church who gravitate toward languages, who spontaneously befriend internationals, who have a gift of loving people for Jesus, who have great compassion for the marginalized, or who are very outgoing and effective in sharing their faith? Are there people who, back from a mission trip, can't get mission out of their minds, who are always wondering if they could do more? Perhaps the team will ask a Godly elder or former missionary to come alongside these people, pray with them and help them look toward a possible vocation in mission?

Although mission organizations provide some equipping and orientation for working cross-culturally, the local church is the best place for potential workers to learn Scripture, be discipled and mentored, get their relationships straightened out, overcome dysfunctional backgrounds, develop relationships with internationals, spend time in needy areas, and practice ministry. Your team can develop an outline or a plan to help people prepare for vocational ministry and to evaluate the growth areas needed for those who desire to go. When people express an interest in mission work, a mentor can help them evaluate their needs and growth areas and work through an appropriate plan.

"Sending New Missionaries" by Ellen Livingood – a packet of downloads for local churches available for purchase, www.catalystservices.org/bm~doc/sendnew.pdf

Skills, Knowledge, Character: A Church-Based Approach to Missionary Candidate Training by Greg Carter

Global Mission Handbook by Steve Hoke and Bill Taylor (Note the chart for assessing growth areas on pp. 44-45.)

To Timbuktu & Beyond: A Guide to Geting Started in Missions by Marsha Woodard

For samples of local church missionary preparation processes, contact DMays@themissionexchange.org.

WORK SPACE:

In our church the following leaders are committed to sending high-quality workers and noticing individuals with appropriate qualities:

___ senior pastor, ___ staff pastors, ___ elders, ___ board members,

___ ministry leaders, ___mission team,

___ others (specify) _____.

It is common in our church for leaders to approach individuals about the possibility of considering vocational mission service. T/F

Our church has a document that describes our expectations and requirements for people who desire to serve as vocational missionaries or workers. T/F

Our church has a written document to help prospective vocational workers evaluate their strengths and growth areas. T/F

Our church has a practical document that describes how we will help prepare, train, and send vocational workers. T/F

Our church helps candidates match up with a mentor who will encourage them, help them deal with difficult issues, and pray for them. T/F

In the past five years our church has helped prepare and send ___ (#) individuals, couples, or families into vocational mission.

Currently in our church ___ (#) individuals, ___ (#) couples, and ___ (#) families are in the process of preparing for a career in mission.

Our team will take the following steps to more effectively recruit, prepare and send vocational workers (person responsible, action step, date):

_____

_____

_____

_____

Sending

The church is interested in both the worker and the church's strategic priorities. Therefore, church leaders and the mission team can help prospective workers consider and evaluate types of ministry, mission organizations, and fields of service in relation to both the worker's call and gifting and the church's priorities. If the individual goes on an independent assignment, for example, as a visiting university teacher or an independent business person, the church can work out individual arrangements for prayer, support, emergencies, and financial assistance as appropriate.

When sending a missionary out of the country, the church has the opportunity to do much more than simply send a check and a few prayers. The missionary is the church's representative, sent to do the church's ministry. This means that the church has a responsibility to do all it can to help make the missionary effective. Because getting established and becoming effective in ministry in another culture is a very arduous and complicated business, the church may have many opportunities.

The missionary is the church's representative, sent to do the church's ministry. This means that the church has a responsibility to do all it can to help make the missionary effective.

Supporting

Almost every missionary and worker will list prayer support first on their list of requests to their friends, supporters, and their home church. People tend to pray for people they love, so helping individuals develop personal relationships with the worker will be invaluable to gaining prayer support. A number of suggestions are available for helping your congregation pray individually. In addition to prayer, support teams may find ways to care for the worker and his or her family personally. Particular times when missionaries need special attention and care are during decision times, the support-raising process, when they first arrive on the field, when difficulties occur, when they transition back to the U.S. for visits or home assignment, when there are family deaths, when there are changes of fields or assignments, and upon permanent return to the U.S.

Serving as Senders by Neal Pirolo

"Help Your Congregation Pray for Missionaries," *Stuff* vol. IV, 37

"How to Pray for Missionaries Daily through the Month," *Stuff* vol. III, 38

"Prayer Support Teams for Your Missionaries," *Stuff* vol. II, 41

Barnabas International, www.barnabas.org

Global Member Care Network, www.globalmembercare.com

Missionary Care Resources for Missions and Mental Health, www.missionarycare.com

But there is an additional opportunity for those who support a worker. And that is to help them in their work. In past generations missionaries were overseas, communications were slow and travel was expensive. Now, the situation is different. A committed congregation can help a local worker in many facets of ministry, even if it is troubleshooting a computer or providing transportation. And with global communication and constant travel, people stateside can find all kinds of ways to help an overseas missionary be more productive. People can do research, obtain corporate discounts on computer programs and equipment, find and ship supplies, and visit on-site to do any manner of construction, repair, or installation of equipment, provide business or medical assistance, and many other things.

WORK SPACE:

Our mission team takes an active role in providing guidance and assistance to prospective missionaries and workers. Specifically, we help them to
- consider appropriate sending organizations. T/F
- discover their best roles. T/F
- identify service avenues that use their spiritual gifts and skills. T/F
- find ministry that fulfills the church's priorities. T/F
- sort out other important factors in getting to the field. T/F

Our church has formal arrangements with, cooperates with, and appropriately supports individuals from our church who are serving overseas in professional, business, or educational roles for purposes of Christian mission. T/F

Each vocational worker our church supports is adequately covered in prayer by several individuals and/or groups who have overtly indicated their commitment. T/F

Each vocational worker from our church is supported emotionally, physically, and vocationally by an identified support team. T/F

It is not uncommon for people or groups from our church to do work on behalf of a vocational missionary or nearby worker: to research something, find something, send something, advise about something, or go assist with something. T/F

The most productive steps we could take to send and support our far-away missionaries more effectively would be:

_____

_____

The most productive steps we could take to send and support nearby vocational workers more effectively would be:

_____

_____

Our team will take the following actions: (person responsible, action step, date):

_____

_____

_____

QUALIFICATIONS AND TRAINING
What do we have to be and know?

Biblical Knowledge

Because the church is responsible to carry out in the world what Jesus commanded us to do, and because the team has a primary responsibility to consider, select, and propose mission work for the church, it is critically important that the team have a clear understanding of the mission priorities of Scripture. If team members are weak, confused, or divided in their understanding of Scripture, the church may invest the majority of its efforts in lesser priorities. In the long run it will accomplish much less than God intends and perhaps leave many desperate people unserved that it could have helped. Further, the team may be poorly equipped to evaluate the strategies, methods, and effectiveness of partners, workers, and their own congregation's involvement.

It is critically important that the team have a clear understanding of the mission priorities of Scripture.

This does not mean that a young Christian or one with little biblical knowledge is disqualified from the team, but such a person must be open and teachable, and there must be a good repository of biblical knowledge in the team to share.

Additional Knowledge

The mission team needs knowledge in a broad spectrum of areas. It is very helpful to know some history of how and where Christianity has spread in the past, particularly the past two centuries. It is quite encouraging and instructive to learn about some of the heroes and pioneers of the modern era of mission. It is very helpful to know where Christianity is expanding and where it is currently very weak. An acquaintance with mission strategies, mission methods, and mission organizations is very useful. The team will learn to recognize and understand mission concepts, terminology, and quite a few acronyms. Of course, being involved globally, the team needs an acquaintance with world geography. In order to understand, sympathize with, pray for, and assist international workers and partners they need a grasp of the complications of working in different cultures and languages. They will benefit from knowing what kinds of ministry can be done effectively by short-term teams and what ministries require long-term workers who give a significant portion of their lives to learning the culture and loving the people. What does the church need to do to help prepare new workers and missionaries prepare for ministry?

The team must become familiar with the purposes and goals of the church.

It is useful to be aware of major world movements, religions, and governments, what they believe, how Christians fare in those areas, the climate for Christian mission, and what kinds of ministries are appropriate and effective. It is important to keep up with world events: wars, natural disasters, rapid growth of systemic sins, changes in regimes—the kinds of changes that signal new opportunities or concerns. Personal relationships with key individuals in a few mission organizations can be very valuable.

Closer to home, the team can learn about the demographics of their city and its communities, some of the urgent needs, what organizations are working where, what other churches are doing, and what strategies seem to be bearing fruit.

Of course, the team must become familiar with the purposes and goals of the church. What are the primary aims of church leaders? How does the church operate in terms of philosophy, policies and procedures? How has mission been handled in the past? Who in the church has knowledge and experience that will be helpful to the team? What mission education and training has been done? What are the current mission policies and practices? What is the history of the mission efforts that the church is currently supporting? How did these originate and why? How is the church changing in regard to its outreach priorities and practices? The team needs to know what mission resources are available and where to find outside help as it is needed. What courses, conferences, seminars, training events, speakers and experts are available? Who in other nearby churches can serve as a resource?

Spiritual Qualities

Perhaps it needs to be said that the people who make up the team must be people who are followers of Jesus and have an urgent desire that others know Jesus. This doesn't mean that everyone on the team must be a senior saint. There is room for young believers to grow. But the ethos of the team must be heavily biased toward bringing people to Christ. If there is divergence in aims, spiritual results will be truncated. Thus the team needs a heavy measure of spiritual maturity and concern for the lost. Team members must understand the biblical and spiritual nature of mission and the total fruitlessness of human efforts without God's intervention. They must be growing in their confidence in and reliance on prayer.

There is a growing wave of compassion among the young that may drive many into mission. This is highly commendable and brings a needed corrective to many mission efforts. At the same time, the evangelistic aspect of ministry must not be neglected.

Other Qualities

A variety of talents, skills, gifts and experiences are needed on the team. Diversity provides a fount of creativity. In many teams the lack of diversity is a great hindrance. A youth on the team can provide insights that older saints may never see on their own. Further, younger people are likely to have the technical skills needed for creating video, artwork, and some kinds of writing. What about someone from another ethnic group? A number of churches are deliberately seeking someone from another culture for their mission pastor.

Diversity provides a fount of creativity.

The team requires someone with leadership characteristics. After all, the team is guiding and helping other leaders to move forward. However, teams do not benefit when a strong personality dominates and everyone else defers. A team may falter or head in a peculiar direction when one voice overrides all others. Team members need large doses of grace, cooperation, teachability, and flexibility. It's good to have some fun. A little levity defuses many tense situations. The team needs a strategic thinker to help the team consider the appropriate possibilities, cautions, and realities. An administrator will keep good records and be sure that commitments are completed and the work is done. The team needs a healthy dose of energetic workers—often in the shortest supply. Creativity is essential for good communication and promotion. Can you recruit someone who is, for example, a graphic designer or a videographer? Select team members from people who are active in church. Pray, watch, and recruit.

The presence of someone who is very relational and an influencer of others will help in recruiting and building relationships with other church departments and ministries. Do you have someone who is a good communicator in the pulpit and a good writer? Look for an expert, someone with mission experience, particularly one who is knowledgeable about a broad spectrum of ministries.

A pastor once told me, "We want people on the team who look like our church." Overall, the team should look a lot like your congregation. If the team is a whole generation older than your congregation, or if it is made up of people who don't seem to fit in your church, you can imagine that it will have a difficult time leading the church in mission.

Some Qualities Needed on the Mission Team

Spiritual maturity	Biblical knowledge	Concern for the lost
Active in church	Mission knowledge	Leadership
Cooperation	Flexibility	Creativity
Time	Strategic Thinker	Visionary
Learners	Administrator	Communicator
Influencer	Workers	Multiple Generations
People like the congregation	Mission experience	Relational
Reader	Technophile	

Training and Educational Opportunities

Preparation and training for the mission team can be formal (for example, college courses), non-formal (organized, short-term learning outside of the formal education system), or informal (life-long learning and on-the job training). Team members may learn on their own and as a group. Some preparation and knowledge will be necessary before a team member can make a significant contribution to the team. However, many individuals may volunteer for specific assignments or task groups and contribute greatly to the team's objectives without becoming a formal member of the team.

Include Bible study, minimally as a devotional, but ideally much more in-depth, individually and as a regular part of team meetings. Encourage individuals to maintain a regular Bible reading time. I have found it useful to highlight every instance where the Bible speaks of God's interest in the nations or the world.

Highlight every instance where the Bible speaks of God's interest in the nations or the world.

Some churches require mission team members and prospective missionaries to take the course, "Perspectives on the World Christian Movement." This course is offered in many cities across the country and is the best lay training in mission available. A lineup of experts presents fifteen sessions covering the biblical basis of mission, the history of the spread of Christianity, the challenges of working across cultures, and strategies God is using in the world today.

Other curricula that the team might study together include "Bridges," a study of how to build relationships with Muslims; "Encountering Islam," a whole course similar to "Perspectives" dealing with understanding and ministering to Muslims; "Cross-Cultural Connections," a curriculum by Mary Lederleitner to introduce Christians to building relationships with people of other cultures based on Duane Elmer's book of the same title; or "Kingdom Expansion 101," an online course on mission by Bruce Camp.

The team may read a mission book between meetings and discuss it when together. It might be a Bible study on mission such as *God's Heart for the Nations* by Jeff Lewis. It could also be a book on global Christianity such as *Kingdom Without Borders, The Untold*

Story of Global Christianity by Miriam Adeney. You might include a mobilization or motivational book such as *Don't Waste Your Life* by John Piper or *Live Life on Purpose* by Claude Hickman. A team can begin to decipher its own *American Cultural Baggage* (by Stan Nussbaum) and understand cultural differences from Sherwood Lingenfelter's *Cross-Cultural Ministry* and from Duane Elmer's *Cross-Cultural Connections.*

Women can learn much about living overseas from *Through Her Eyes* by Marti Smith, a series of extensive interviews with women missionaries. Christine Mallouhi provides a great deal of insight on how to dress to show respect in the Muslim world in *Miniskirts, Mothers and Muslims.* The team can begin to comprehend partnership difficulties from *Cross-Cultural Partnerships* by Mary Lederleitner and obtain extremely interesting insights on how relationships, finances and security are viewed in much of Africa from David Maranz' *African Friends and Money Matters.* You might include a book on humanitarian ministries relating to immigration, justice, human trafficking, poverty, etc. *When Helping Hurts* by Steve Corbett & Brian Fikkert is an excellent study. A missionary biography can be a powerful inspiration. For example, try *Living Sacrifice* by Dr. Helen Roseveare. Someone could read a book or find information on the web on global trends and report to the group. Team members may subscribe to *Mission Frontiers,* the *Global Prayer Digest,* or other mission periodicals.

There are a variety of conferences and seminars that are very worthwhile. The triennial Urbana Student Mission Conference is the premier event. ACMC conferences are held in various cities across the country. They specialize in workshops that provide practical help to local churches in mission. The North American Mission Leaders Conference is held annually in September. This conference has traditionally served mission organization leaders but is expanding its format to serve local churches as well. There are a growing number of national and regional conferences addressing various types of ministry. Individuals may enroll for extension courses from universities.

The team may watch mission videos or participate in live or recorded webinars from The Mission Exchange. For example, recorded webinars are available on support-raising, missionary care, mobilizing professionals for mission, spiritual formation of missionaries, mission education for children, and many other important topics. Expose the team to videos, links, and statistics on

WORK SPACE:

Our team would benefit from additional knowledge in the following areas:

_____

_____

We will take these steps to improve in this area (action step, person responsible and date):

_____

_____

_____

Our team would benefit by the addition of the following skills, gifts, talents and experience: _____

_____

_____

web sites. Invite a missionary, a believer from another country or another religious background, a special speaker or a consultant to address your group. Ask team members to host a visiting missionary. Go to a mall and observe shoppers with a view to discerning cultural values. Go as a team to visit an ethnic neighborhood or a mosque or to do a community work project and then get together to debrief. Encourage team members to develop a cross-cultural relationship. Provide opportunities for team members to participate in a mission trip to get first-hand exposure.

We will take these steps to recruit people with these qualities (action step, person responsible and date):

_____

_____

_____

_____

Our team would benefit from the following educational and training activities:

_____

_____

_____

We will take the following steps to conduct these training activities (person responsible, action step, date):

_____

_____

_____

CONSTITUENCIES
With whom do we work?

Constituencies are the individuals and groups with which the mission team does business, both within and outside the local church. The mission team interfaces with a broad variety of church leaders and groups. The team's aim for these constituencies is for every leader, every ministry, every group, and every individual to learn about, commit to, and get practically involved in reaching the world for Christ—global mission. Global mission, of course, includes both our nation and the other nations.

Ideally the mission team becomes the resource team, equipping every ministry in the church to participate in mission.

Why, you may ask, should the team expect every other ministry to get involved in "our ministry"? The answer is that reaching the world for Christ is part of the purpose of the church. Many would say it is the overarching mission of the church. The mission of the whole is the mission of the parts. Or, said another way, the purpose of the church is the purpose of every ministry and individual in the church. Thus it is the responsibility of every leader, every department, every ministry, every group, and every individual to contribute to the purpose, or mission, of discipling the nations. Your aim, therefore, is to help each constituency understand this fact, learn about world mission, commit to it, and get involved.

Ideally, the mission team becomes the resource team, not doing mission on behalf of the church, but equipping every ministry in the church to participate in outreach and mission. Some individuals will go long-term somewhere else in the world; some will go short-term; some will minister full-time locally; some will minister on an ongoing volunteer basis locally, and the remainder will live as salt and light, witnessing and serving where they live and work, in their homes, neighborhoods, schools, and work places – and learning about, praying for, and supporting those who go.

 Becoming a World-Changing Church by David Mays

Senior Pastor

The senior pastor is a key player in everything that is top priority in the church. Your desire and prayer is that your pastor seeks to build a world vision into the life of every member. In many churches the senior pastor leads the charge to mobilize the congregation to reach the community and the world for Christ. The pastor demonstrates an authentic, persistent, and powerful urgency for mission. The pastor participates in developing the vision and strategy for mission. The pastor preaches on mission, takes a public leadership position in mission events, personally knows one or several missionaries and supports them in prayer and friendship, occasionally travels to ministry locations, and personally promotes mission and recruits individuals to be involved.

The mission team dreams of having a pastor like the 30-year founding pastor of Briarwood Presbyterian Church in Birmingham. It was said of Frank Barker that if you wanted to convince him of some new project, program or initiative, you had to demonstrate to him how it would help the church reach the world for Christ. He had a plaque in his office that read, "...so that we can reach the world for Christ."

In other churches the senior pastor delegates mission to another pastor or the mission team. In either case, the mission team can look for opportunities to stimulate mission vision by providing tactful and helpful mission encouragement in the form of conversations, articles (with the most powerful sections highlighted), books (with pertinent passages marked), video clips, prayer requests, etc. The pastor can be invited to take a minor but visible leadership role in mission events. Periodically the pastor can be encouraged to represent the church on a mission trip.

Your desire and prayer is that your pastor will seek to build a world vision into the life of every member.

Pray for your pastors consistently. Pray for their growth in godliness, their family, their relationships, their preaching, their vision for the church, and their heart for the nations. An appropriate person from your team can become the pastor's friend, meeting together periodically and listening, encouraging, praying, and stimulating a greater depth of world vision.

It's more important to get on your pastor's team than to get him on your team.

Remember this tip I learned years ago from a pastor. "It's more important to get on your pastor's team than to get the pastor on your team." Pastors have many critics. Become a fan. Catch the pastor doing something you like and write a thank you note.

WORK SPACE:

Our senior pastor furthers the cause of mission in our church in the following ways:

_____

_____

_____

_____

For our senior pastor, global mission is (in my judgment)

_____ The number one priority

_____ One of the top three priorities

_____ One of several important priorities

_____ Important (as long as it doesn't interfere with a higher priority)

_____ Not very important

The most important thing I would like to see our pastor do in regard to mission is

_____

_____

The relationship of the mission team with the senior pastor could be best described as:

_____

_____

We will attempt to assist and encourage our senior pastor, both in mission and in life and ministry by (person responsible, action step, date):

_____

_____

_____

Staff Pastors and Ministry Leaders

Very likely your church has more than one pastor, perhaps a youth pastor, a children's pastor, a worship pastor, and others. In fact, one way to perceive a church's priorities is to examine what ministries and efforts are led directly by a pastor. If you do not have multiple pastors, these ministries and others have lay leaders. There is good reason for the mission team to be involved with each one. First of all, the team desires to help these leaders strengthen their own vision for and commitment to mission. Secondly, the mission team desires to assist all leaders in incorporating mission education and mission involvement in their own ministries.

Perhaps the worship leader is in the best position in the church to keep God's heart for the nations in front of the congregation.

Perhaps the worship leader is in the best position in the church to keep God's heart for all nations in the minds of the congregation. The worship leader, every week, leads the congregation in singing the praises of the one great God who created the universe and everything in it, who gave his life to redeem his creation, and who longs that all nations worship him. Although in every worship service we sing wonderful words that express these thoughts in an amazing variety of ways, we often miss the import of the words. The worship leader has the opportunity to bring to the congregation's attention the meaning and implications of what we sing. I recently read of a worship leader who, after leading music about God's greatness and His desire for the nations, would then bring to the attention of the people through pictures and statistics the condition of some as yet unreached people group for prayer.

In many churches each department is asked to submit a six-month plan and provide a six-month evaluation. The mission team can serve a variety of ministries such as the children's ministry, the youth ministry, small groups, and other ministries by recommending educational resources and potential projects and partners to include in their six-month plan. As needed, the team may also provide experienced volunteers or teachers to help implement the plan. A six-month plan could include either 1) education about or 2) involvement with

- a. people like us nearby,
- b. people unlike us nearby, or
- c. people unlike us far away.

Six possible combinations of the above would cover a three-year time frame. So, for example, in one six-month period, a ministry might study the history, culture, and spiritual state of the Burmese (1c above). In another period, the ministry might spend time developing relationships with the local Burmese refugee community (2b). And so on.

Consider three kinds of people: people like us nearby, people unlike us nearby and people unlike us far away.

If some ministry leaders do not include mission as suggested above, the mission team may be able to serve their interests in other ways. Perhaps the team can identify individuals they know within these ministries who have a commitment to mission and will volunteer, with team help, to find ways to incorporate mission in their particular group or ministry. One possible avenue is to volunteer to lead a devotional for a series of meetings using the

Global Prayer Digest or a devotional that follows the theme of God's heart for the nations in Scripture.

Building Global Minded Christians by Mark Mays, www.davidmays.org/Resources/Building_Global_Minded_Christians.pdf

Church Board

The relationship between the team and the church governing body is particularly important for several reasons. The board (or session) not only oversees and approves all ministries and budgets, but also has overall leadership responsibility for the church. As with any group in the church, mission knowledge and passion may vary broadly among board members. Further, whereas the results or lack of results in other areas of ministry may be directly observable by board members, the mission work of the church may not be directly visible within the church. The board must be kept informed of what the mission team and other church groups are planning and doing in mission. One of the best ways is for a member of the board to serve on the mission team. In this way, the mission team can also be kept in the loop on church priorities and aims.

The team can periodically request opportunities to make reports to the board in regard to mission priorities, ministry updates or potential goals. The team can also offer occasional brief mission updates to the board on trends, strategies, global or local updates, and church opportunities. In the ideal scenario, over time, the church board and the church staff are discipled in the biblical mandate of mission by the senior pastor.

WORK SPACE:

A member of the church governing board serves on our mission team. T/F

The mission team, or its representative, meets with and informs the board at least quarterly. T/F

Our team feels that our board is well informed of our ministry priorities and direction for mission in our church: 1 (no) 2   3   4   5 (yes)

Our team feels that we are well informed of the board's ministry priorities and direction for the future: 1 (no) 2   3   4   5 (yes)

Our team could improve our communication with the church board by:

_____

_____

_____

_____

Our team will take the following steps (person responsible, action step, date):

_____

_____

_____

_____

Missionaries – Long-Term, Far Away

The team has an obvious responsibility toward the church's sent or supported offsite mission workers. The responsibility extends toward the missionary on behalf of the church and toward the church on behalf of the missionary. The team represents the church in keeping abreast of the missionary's work, goals, methods, hopes, progress, successes, failures, and needs. If the church has sent the missionary, the church carries considerable responsibility to ensure the missionary has the resources needed for the work, is properly supervised, has good relationships with co-workers and national Christians, has appropriate development opportunities, is growing, is effective, is healthy, and is cared for. It is helpful to delegate some of this ministry—especially that of supplemental provision, assistance and care for the missionary—to individuals and groups in the church.

Each missionary may have an advocate in the church who serves as the key communicator between church and missionary. Even better is to have a team of people behind each missionary. In some churches small groups, adult Bible fellowships, or Sunday School classes adopt missionaries for this purpose. In others, a collection of interested individuals become the support team. Some churches have guidelines and suggestions for support teams.

Even better is to have a team of people behind each missionary.

The team is also responsible to keep the missionary informed about progress and changes in the church, encouraging the missionary by how God is at work back home. The team will keep the missionary up to date regarding the church's mission activities, aims, and direction, and particularly changes in priorities and strategies in mission. It can be very helpful (and respectful) to obtain the missionaries' insights and concerns in advance regarding significant changes.

The mission team is also responsible to communicate with the congregation on behalf of the missionary. The missionary is a church delegate carrying out the church's ministry on behalf of the congregation. It is proper that the congregation be kept informed of how "their" ministry is going, to rejoice over victories, pray over difficulties, and help with needs. What is God doing? Where are people being helped and coming to Christ and the church growing? What is the climate for ministry? Where is Satan hindering? How is the situation changing? What roadblocks are encountered? What are the threats and opportunities? What needs are springing up? Where does the missionary need God's direction and the church's encouragement? What resources does the missionary need? How can the church help?

"Support Team Leader Job Description," *Stuff* vol. IV, 52

"Prayer Support Team for Your Missionaries," *Stuff* vol. II, 41

For sample missionary care programs from individual churches, contact David Mays at DMays@TheMissionExchange.org.

Mission Workers – Short-Term or Nearby

The mission team has similar responsibilities for other workers, but in many cases to a lesser degree. Nearby workers can sometimes maintain their regular communication channels and support groups and attend church frequently. Those on mission trips need concentrated prayer during their preparation and while they are gone and opportunities to speak to groups when they return. The team is responsible for adequate follow through.

Partners

Growing and maintaining effective partnerships can be trying, requiring considerable understanding, diplomacy and grace. "Effective, lasting partnering initiatives need a committed facilitator. The facilitator must bring the partnership to life and keep the fires burning, demonstrating patience, tenacity, vision, and the spirit of a servant. This prophet, servant, and resource person needs training, nurturing, and encouragement. ... An effective, durable partnering initiative is a process, not an event. Every lasting partnership has exploration, formation, and operation stages. Forming them usually takes much more time than expected. The quickest way to kill a partnership is to call a meeting! Build personal relationships; get to know the potential partners, the priority issues, and the perceived roadblocks. Doing this will produce huge dividends later."[8]

An effective, durable partnering initiative is a process, not an event.

The Great Commission Community

Church mission leaders have multiple opportunities to connect with, contribute to, and learn from a variety of peers, practitioners, mentors, experts, resource persons, leaders, and organizations in the Great Commission community. The team can learn from blogs, vlogs, web sites, pamphlets, periodicals, books, seminars, conferences, coaching sessions, and any number of other venues provided by people and organizations experienced in mission. Church leaders can meet their peers in other churches in their city and elsewhere. A variety of church mission consultants are available. Global mission is a multi-faceted team effort from everywhere to everywhere by the global church. Your church and your team are part of that global effort.

Great Commission Community Connections

ACMC (Advancing Churches in Missions Commitment), www.ACMC.org
Catalyst Services, Ellen Livingood, www.catalystservices.org
Cross-Global Link, www.crossgloballink.org
David Mays, www.DavidMays.org
DualReach, Bruce Camp, www.dualreach.org
Local Mission Pastor Networks
Mission mobilization, consulting, sending and support organizations
Sixteen:Fifteen Church Missions Coaching, www.1615.org
The Mission Exchange, www.TheMissionExchange.org
The National Association of Mission Pastors
The US Center for World Mission, www.uscwm.org
Your denomination mission board

WORK AREA:

Our connections with the Great Commission Community include the following:

_____
_____
_____

We have utilized these connections in the following ways:

_____
_____

Our church and our mission ministry would benefit by being connected in the following areas:

_____
_____

Our church and our mission ministry would benefit by being connected with the following organizations:

_____
_____

We will take the following steps to get connected (person responsible, action step, date):

_____
_____

STRUCTURE
How do we organize ourselves?

The best structure for your team depends upon the amount of work you need to do, the size of the team, how you recruit and use volunteers, and how your church operates. In the simplest case of a small church, the mission "team" may simply be one person who handles the mission responsibility. This might be the pastor or it could be a board member or layperson. The church perhaps has limited mission involvement and the "mission person" does what one person can do.

Mission Team

In many churches the mission team was formerly called a committee. Becoming a team means becoming workers together instead of being primarily idea-generators or decision-makers. Individual team members assume responsibility for particular functions of the team or areas of ministry and do most of the work outside team meetings. So, for example, one team member might assume responsibility for communicating mission to the congregation. A second person might lead a group volunteering in a homeless shelter. A third person might serve as facilitator or intermediary for a partnership. Someone might oversee the care and support of missionaries. Another person might oversee administration of finances. And so on.

Sub-Teams

When the mission ministry becomes too large for one person to handle a whole area of responsibility, that person recruits additional individuals to assist in carrying out the assigned responsibilities. Those recruited become part of sub-teams or task groups that may or may not be members of the mission team. Sub-teams may meet regularly or periodically with the mission team or they may meet at another time. They may meet irregularly, or not at all, communicating as needed by email and telephone.

In some churches, sub-teams or task groups assume functional roles as above. In other churches, sub-team responsibilities may take responsibility for a geographic area such as a continent, a city, or your community; a more localized area of church mission involvement; a partner; or an individual worker. Or a combination is possible. For example, a church might have one sub-team responsible for Africa, one for an orphanage in Brazil, one to handle video communication with the church, one for organizing mission trips, and one facilitating their partnership with an inner city ministry.

Multiple Teams

In some churches, a sub-team responsible for a continent, ministry area, partnership or mission function, may be elevated to a full team and given authority and financial responsibility (within the approved budget) for that area of ministry. Thus the church could have several mission teams, all reporting to a steering group or mission pastor. One church has separate teams for global mission, local ethnic mission, and local same culture mission. Each team is lead by a staff member. These teams are sometimes called regional teams, impact teams, or task forces.

One church has seven teams, each responsible for a region of the world. The seven team leaders and the mission pastor make up a steering team. Once the budget is determined, each regional team has authority for managing funds for their region. Each team also has responsibility for assessing needs, developing partner relationships, establishing strategy, and overseeing ministry for their region. The regional teams become experts in their ministry areas.

Another church modeled their mission ministry after the youth ministry. Everyone who contributes to the youth ministry on a regular basis—whether bringing cookies, teaching a class, or helping organize a youth trip—is called a youth ministry volunteer. Similarly in mission, the mission pastor recruited champions for various ministry areas. He charged each champion with developing the support volunteers needed for that area. So the champion for mission trips recruited someone to do the screening and evaluation of candidates for all mission trips, someone to oversee all the training, someone to handle planning and logistics, someone to handle follow through. These individuals recruited additional volunteers where they needed help. For example, one person volunteered to teach each group how to pack for a trip. Another champion agreed to oversee all missionary care. That champion recruited an individual to be the point person for each missionary. The missionary care person did not have to do any paperwork for the mission team or sit in on any meetings.

One church had more than 140 people serving in mission leadership.

At one time this church, which had never sent a missionary, had twenty missionary families in the pipeline. Preparation of these missionaries was a big deal. The mission pastor recruited a champion for "candidacy." While the mission pastor headed up the screening and selection process, the champion recruited volunteers for development and mentoring, and transition teams to help new missionaries move to the field. In this church an administrative team handled strategy, budgets, and other high level issues. The remainder of the ministry in twelve categories was carried about by more than 100 volunteers led by individual champions. The champion of each general area reported to the mission pastor. The church had more than 140 people serving in mission leadership.[9]

Some churches encourage any individual with a passion for a particular ministry to initiate, recruit, and form a ministry team (sometimes called an impact team or task force) and to champion and lead the team. These ministry teams associate with the mission team and exist under its authority, but may take initiative and operate largely autonomously. Some churches ask them to fund their own ministries. One church advised, "Go ahead. Start your own ministry. Just don't do anything illegal or immoral; stay away from heresy; and don't ask for money."

Alternative Structures

Some churches have a steering team (or executive team) of three to six people. The steering team might include a pastor, the mission chairman, an elder, and an in-house mission expert. It meets separately and handles the 30,000-foot issues. It may provide the general direction and priorities for the mission team, prepare the budget, and handle higher level personnel issues. The mission team serves the executive team by providing input, giving feedback and implementing the operations. In staff-led churches, a pastor, with input from the pastoral staff, may guide the process. The pastor may oversee a mission team or relate directly to task forces or impact teams and individuals or small groups who carry out various functions.

Diagrams of Team Structures:

TEAM

**TEAM AND
SUB-TEAMS**
Sub-team members are also
part of the team

**TEAM AND
SUB-TEAMS**
Sub-team members are not
part of the team

**EXECUTIVE or
STEERING TEAM**
With mission team
and sub-teams

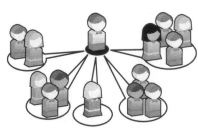

**PASTOR or
CHAIRMAN**
Supported by individuals and
sub-teams

EXECUTIVE TEAM
With regional teams
or task groups

WORK AREA:

A diagram of the structure of our mission team:

The advantages of this structure are:

_____

_____

_____

The disadvantages of this structure are:

_____

_____

_____

A better structure for our mission team might be:

(Description or diagram here.)

This would be a better structure for us because:

_____

_____

OPERATION
How do we execute?

Leadership

The mission team may be chaired by a pastor, a board member, or a layperson. The mission policy may state how the chairperson is to be selected, or a church pastor may select the leader. It may be a formal process or an informal assignment. The team leader may have more or less responsibility for decision-making on the team, or decisions may be made by vote or informal consensus, based largely on general church operating philosophy and habits. In staff-led churches, pastors make most of the important decisions, including who leads the mission team. In board-led churches, decisions are often made more by policy. The chairperson recruits and screens team members, calls for meetings, leads the meetings, arbitrates disagreements, limits discussion, facilitates decision-making, oversees planning, assigns work, and keeps things on track.

The Mission Pastor

The church may have a pastor assigned to mission. Mission may be this pastor's full-time responsibility or just part of the job. Many mission pastors have mission and .... Examples include mission and adult ministries, mission and assimilation, mission and youth, mission and worship. The individual may be responsible for local and global mission or just local or just global. In large churches, the mission pastor may have additional staff support. One church has a pastor for global mission and staff directors for local cross-cultural mission and local same-culture mission. The global mission pastor oversees all three areas.

A mission pastor may lead the mission team or serve as an advisor to the team. Mission pastors (if they have support staff) may assume the paperwork and coordination functions of the team, or they may ask the team to handle these functions. For more on the role of a mission pastor see Appendix I.

Team Meetings

Meetings are often the bottleneck for a variety of reasons. The team tries to do too much and the meetings get long and boring. People feel they are wasting their time and not contributing with their skills. They allow other events to take priority over attending the meetings. Meetings may become infrequent and mission lags in the church. In any number of cases over the years a pastor has admitted to me that his mission team hasn't met for several months and is no longer considered functional. In such cases a team must be restarted, sometimes from scratch.

How can you oversee a global marketing operation on one meeting a month?

One solution is to meet more frequently. Teams should meet as often as needed to accomplish their aims. The most common interval of meetings is monthly, frequently skipping a month or two in the summer. If this is the only mission meeting it seems inadequate for what may be the most important responsibility of the church. As someone has said, "How can you oversee a global marketing operation on one meeting a month?"

In most churches the worship team meets weekly. So it's not out of the bounds of reason for a mission team to meet weekly. And if the mission team experienced as much fellowship, joy and fulfillment in their meetings as many worship teams do, a weekly meeting might thrive. If you only need one meeting a month, reconsider whether you are carrying out all your responsibilities.

At the same time, meetings are problematic. Everyone is busy. Family and work conflicts arise. People are out of town and out of the country. Other priorities seem more urgent on any given day. This adds pressure to leaders to make meetings significant, worthwhile, productive, and enjoyable. In many church ministries a natural sense of camaraderie and community develops that encourages participation. One mission leader told me their team functioned well when there was a lot of communication among team members outside the meeting.

Meetings are necessary but they are not the core activity of mission teams. Another solution is to hold fewer meetings and maximize them by pushing much of the content elsewhere. Move work down to subgroups or task teams and push most decisions up to a steering team or pastor or down to subgroups or task teams. The smaller groups or task teams can communicate in smaller meetings or informally as needed to keep the work going. If the mission team focuses primarily on learning, vision casting, and reporting, it can meet as often as necessary to keep the learning going, the vision growing and the work flowing.

Prayer focused on the agenda may allow God to open minds and attitudes to his guidance and avoid a great deal of fruitless arguing.

People appreciate meetings that begin on time, end on time, meet in a setting that is comfortable, follow a clear agenda provided in advance, allow appropriate but not interminable discussion, focus on progress and results, and exhibit an ethos that is significant but enjoyable. The team that spends time together in social and fun activities outside the meeting will develop a sense of community.

Prayer is an important part of every meeting. Everyone believes that prayer is the central source of power and guidance, but it is easy to neglect or minimize it. Further, prayer focused on the agenda may allow God to open minds and attitudes to his guidance and help avoid a great deal of fruitless arguing.

Perhaps every meeting could include some brief consideration of what God is telling us in the Bible. This is a form of both education and inspiration. Maybe each meeting could also include some other form of education, whether it is a geography quiz, a report on a missionary biography, a summary of a web article, a personal experience in mission, or a conversation about a book everyone is reading. The meeting is an appropriate time for significant reports from or about one or more missionaries, partners, projects, ministries, countries, or people groups.

The meeting also relates to the work of the team, doing *or delegating* each of the following: reporting on progress for each initiative or objective; rescheduling delayed actions; considering new items, requests, and needs; making necessary decisions or recommendations; brainstorming new initiatives; planning for upcoming events; setting new objectives and plans; and assigning work.

Getting the Work Done

The work is done primarily between meetings by those individuals or task groups who agreed to do it, with the help of others they recruit as needed. Each larger goal has individual action steps with deadlines, and each responsible individual reports on progress at each meeting. If a step is not completed when it is due, the person responsible establishes the new date at which it will be completed and adjusts the schedule appropriately.

Mission Planning Worksheet

Responsibility Area: _____

Goal: _____

Person responsible: _____

To be completed by: _____

Next Step:_____By: _____

Responsibility Area: _____

Goal: _____

Person responsible: _____

To be completed by: _____

Next Step:_____By: _____

Responsibility Area: _____

Goal: _____

Person responsible: _____

To be completed by: _____

Next Step:_____By: _____

Finances

At each meeting, a report of the financial situation is given by the person responsible for tracking finances. Deviations from the budget are explained, and any necessary adjustments are discussed. New requests are considered, and decisions or recommendations are made to the church board as appropriate. In the fall of each year, the team or designated group puts together a proposed budget for the following year and submits it to the church board.

Retreats and Planning Sessions

An annual strategy retreat or planning session can be of great benefit to orient new team members, build community, motivate the team, learn from Scripture or other sources, pray together, and especially to plan for the future. It is a good time to evaluate and realign. In a retreat of at least a half day, and preferably a weekend, extended time can be given to considering the future. An outside facilitator with experience in local church mission can help the team take a fresh look at the church's current operation and mission plan, obtain direction from Scripture, consider changes in the world and mission trends in churches, and help the team think through possibilities and set fresh goals. Consider inviting the church board to participate in the retreat, or part of it, to get a much more in-depth perspective of the value, roles, and potential for the church in mission.

Periodically the church may conduct a major re-visioning process for mission. It may take several sessions. Establishing new aims or priorities requires the involvement of top church leaders. Significant changes in direction will only be maintained when top church leaders help establish the direction and commit to it.

"Format for a Half-Day Missions Retreat," *Stuff* vol. IV, 24
"Missions Retreat Evaluation," *Stuff* vol. IV, 26

WORK SPACE:

Our team is led by ___ the senior pastor, ___ a staff pastor,

___ the mission pastor, ___ a board member, ___ another lay leader.

We have a ___ full-time, ___ half-time, ___ part-time,

___ no mission pastor.

Our team meets ___ monthly, ___ semi-monthly, ___ weekly,

___ irregularly, ___ not for a while.

The people on our mission team know each other personally and

enjoy good camaraderie and community. 1 (poor) to 5 (great)

Our mission team meetings are generally well attended.

1 (poor) to 5 (great)

Our mission teams are productive, enjoyable, and significant.

1 (poor) to 5 (great)

During each meeting we spend significant time in prayer.

1 (poor) to 5 (great)

WORK SPACE:

During our meetings we ___ study the Scripture, ___ study a book together, ___ have some other mission education activity.

The majority of the work gets done between the meetings.

1 (poor) to 5 (great)

We have a planning meeting or retreat

___ annually, ___ periodically, ___ no.

The most important steps we could take to improve our

operation would be:

_____

_____

_____

Our team will take the following steps (person responsible,

action step, date):

_____

_____

_____

_____

APPENDIX I:
Critical Roles of the Mission Pastor

The mission pastor has many responsibilities, but some of them are critical. In cooperation with other church leaders, the mission pastor must do the following:

- Shape and promote the premises and purposes for mission in the church.
- Determine and communicate the definition and scope of mission for your church.
- Develop and pursue particular priorities within the larger scope of mission.
- Identify and develop partnerships for accomplishing your mission priorities.
- Manage short-term missions so they contribute to your ongoing mission priorities, encourage long-term missionaries, and develop participants.
- Continually educate church leaders and the congregation regarding the biblical foundation and imperative for mission.
- Assist other church leaders in providing mission education and hands-on ministry opportunities as part of their ministries.
- Recruit, educate, develop, and organize lay leadership teams to assist in leading the mission ministry in areas such as
    - o   Prayer for mission
    - o   Congregational education and promotion
    - o   Worker recruitment, training, and care
    - o   Coordination of projects and partnerships
    - o   Budgeting and finance management

- Encourage sacrificial commitment to cross-cultural ministry.
- Continually study and communicate changes in the world, the culture, the church, and mission.
- Provide assistance and coaching to churches without mission pastors.

"Helps for Missions Pastors," www.DavidMays.org/Missionspastor.html

APPENDIX II:
The Missional Church and Mission

Churches have traditionally sent trained missionaries to other countries, languages, and cultures. Missional churches are justifiably dissatisfied with sending a few people to "do missions" while the great majority simply "do church." They aim to remove the "silo" of missions and send all believers, like missionaries, into both local and global communities. Instead of a small minority doing "missions" as representatives of the church, everyone should be serving in "mission." The church itself is sent. Further, the sending is not only to proclaim and evangelize but to minister and serve in the name of Jesus.

Issues that arise out of this paradigm shift have to do with setting priorities, budgeting, and tracking progress. On the one hand, it might be argued that these things don't matter because it's all "mission." But on the other hand, if there are no guidelines, then the most visible need, the most persistent voice, or the person with the greatest influence directs funding, personnel, and support. And some of the most needy and desperate people are not represented and never served. If all outreach and service activities are lumped together, it raises the question of how to ensure that less visible but strategic ministries and pockets of people out of reach of the Gospel receive an appropriate share of the resources.

There is a sub-current among missional churches that seeks to maximize congregational involvement at the expense of representative mission, as if the former is good but the latter is bad. The church wants to send more people into ministry abroad on mission trips (and more people into the community on mission) and, at the same time, reduce—or at least not add to—the number of full-time "representative" missionaries. Further, the church will not support or connect with an overseas ministry unless volunteers from their church can be involved on-site.

The downside is that some of the most crucial ministry to the least served in the most difficult places in the world cannot be done by American volunteers. It is important to keep our priorities straight. While involvement in mission does benefit the doer (and the church), that is not the purpose for doing mission. We do mission primarily because God desires for us to help people who need it, and we do it in the way that is most effective and beneficial for them. We do not do mission primarily for the benefit of the people who do it or for the church that is doing it or in the way that is most beneficial for us.

If a church desires to faithfully steward its resources and maximize its impact in the world, some kind of categorization and prioritization would seem helpful. Families and institutions establish budgets to ensure a wise and sustainable distribution of resources. Budget categories are established particularly for areas that might naturally be neglected (such as charitable giving) or overspent (such as entertainment).

Churches establish a mission budget—and often do special fund-raising—to ensure a healthy investment of resources to reach, disciple, and help people with little access to Christian resources. In the past, such people were thought of as being in other countries. Increasingly, we are recognizing the needs of our own communities.

If categories were to be assigned within mission, how would you decide what might they be? Here are some questions to consider?

1. Does this opportunity require church financial investment, or can we deploy volunteers or use our facility?

2. Does this opportunity require church leaders to plan, organize, recruit, and lead, or can we encourage individuals to volunteer on their own?

3. Does this opportunity serve primarily
    a. people like us nearby
    b. people unlike us nearby, or
    c. people unlike us far away?

4. Does this opportunity occur in an area rich in churches and Christian resources or among people with a dearth of churches and Christian resources?

Fixed Assets and Portable Assets

Our tendency is to think of church resources in terms of dollars. Money is a portable asset, as is prayer. It can easily be deployed anywhere in the world. However, we also have substantial fixed assets, including our facilities and most of our people. For the most part they can be deployed only locally.

In order to maximize and balance the use of our resources, it helps to think of using *fixed* resources locally and *portable* assets farther away. Therefore, as much as possible, we can deploy our people as volunteers in every kind of local situation and ministry, supported as needed by minimal funds. The more we deploy people locally and use dollars globally, the greater our potential impact. Alternatively, the more dollars we spend locally, the less we can accomplish globally.

Institutional or Individual Initiative

An institutional initiative could be represented by something like adopting a sister city, adopting an unreached people group, providing facilities for a community recreation league, sponsoring a home for battered women, or partnering with a local school.

An individual initiative could be represented by someone who takes an overseas job with a multinational company, someone who applies to serve overseas with a mission organization, someone who independently goes on a mission trip, a person who volunteers at the local rescue mission, an individual who serves on the board of a mission organization, or someone who shows the love of Jesus to his colleagues, coworkers, and neighbors.

The more church leaders can build an atmosphere of everyone reaching out in their normal sphere of influence and volunteering in the community, the greater the potential impact. Church leaders have limited capacity for planning, organizing, leading, and supervising outside initiatives.

Institutional initiatives will almost always require church staff support and funding. Personal involvement that requires no church funding is almost unlimited in potential opportunities and the amount of good that can be accomplished. In addition, volunteers may often provide personal funds to support ministry.

People like us nearby. People unlike us nearby. People unlike us far away.

The world can be roughly divided in these three categories. The reason for considering these categories is that often one is neglected by a local church. Some churches have focused on global mission while neglecting local evangelism and service. Some churches have focused on helping people in their community while ignoring the larger world. In the past couple of decades, many churches have become increasingly aware of the growing marginalized people in their own communities: ethnic minorities, refugees, the physically challenged, the illiterate, victims of human trafficking, the inner city poor, and many other subgroups.

In considering these categories, a church can ask, "Are we blind to one of these categories of people or giving it less attention than it deserves?" The further away and the more unlike us, the more difficult and expensive it is for us to minister to them. The closer and more like us, the more we can train and deploy our own people at minimal cost. A huge opportunity for the missional church is to send people into their own workplaces, neighborhoods and communities as Jesus' ambassadors at little cost to the church while continuing to maintain a substantial ministry abroad.

Priorities

With these factors in mind we can develop a set of priority statements culminating in a set of goals and a tracking system.

Here are some sample priority statements:

- We will proactively mentor and equip our people to serve as Jesus' ambassadors and witnesses where they live and work.
- We will mentor and equip our people to understand, love, and serve various categories of people unlike us.
- We will deploy our people as ambassadors and volunteers in our community and city, encouraging them to minister at their own expense and provide personal funding to support their ministry as they feel led.
- We will carefully select and establish a few church initiatives to benefit both the community and the larger world for Christ.
- We will encourage, train, and support qualified individuals from our church to serve cross-culturally in strategic and needy areas of the world, including but not limited to our city.
- We will monitor our efforts and resources to ensure that we are appropriately serving our own culture, our community, and the world.

APPENDIX III:
The Poor, The Hurting, The Lost

Since the Asian Tsunami in 2004, followed by Hurricane Katrina in 2005, compassion efforts throughout the world have escalated dramatically. Compassion and justice have become major causes for our culture. People respond to human need. And ministries of compassion are the fastest growing segment of Protestant mission. Missionaries recognized a long time ago that, like Jesus, we love and serve people "without strings attached."

There is a spiritual spectrum among those who minister to human need. At the secular end, there is genuine, well-meaning concern for the welfare of people but little awareness, knowledge or concern for new life in Christ. At the Christian end of the spectrum, there is a deep and genuine concern for the spiritual life and health of people as well as for their physical and social welfare. Real life in Christ is recognized as the crucial, overriding need. How overt or subtle this spiritual concern is expressed may vary dramatically with the context, but that's a different topic.

The issue of interest here is for those in between, those who are Christians but for whom spiritual issues are a low priority. We know that the Gospel transforms culture, but we recognize also that Christianity is shaped by the culture. Perhaps some, if not many, Christians have absorbed the cultural perspective that life is pretty much all about this life, that spiritually, everyone is OK. Spiritual life may be considered significant, but a free, healthy, and productive life here and now is the primary focus of concern.

For some evangelicals, new life in Christ is losing priority. We just don't think about it that much. Physical life confronts us minute-by-minute, while spiritual life seems vague and distant. Perhaps many are driving under their own steam and are more or less unaware of the life-giving power and joy of a relationship with Jesus. Some doubt that life is eternal. Some may assume that coming to know Jesus is not a requirement but simply an added bonus.

Our secular culture assumes that everyone will end up in Heaven, if there is a Heaven. A philosophy of tolerance says that we should not interfere in someone's religion. Asking people to commit to follow Jesus is like recruiting them to your political party, or your church. Proselytizing is bad. Helping people *and* encouraging them to come to Jesus is considered manipulation.

What happens if our missionaries lose their deep concern about the eternal destiny of those they go to help? How will we know? Perhaps we can hear clues as we listen to them. What stories do they tell? When they "light up," what are they talking about? What are their deepest desires for the people they touch? What do they point to as success? What do they consider failure? What breaks their hearts? Perhaps they serve among people where it is dangerous or inflammatory to speak openly of Christ. If so, do they yearn for people to discover the life-giving Savior?

For decades I have heard missionaries tell their stories. Almost always, they have told of helping people with their needs. And almost always, I have heard their longings for these people to know Jesus, to experience new, abundant, eternal life in Christ. When I hear missionaries today, I listen for their heartbeat.

As evangelicals we understand that people who don't know Jesus do not have life. The ultimate issue—as important as it and as much as we care—is not whether this life is difficult, but what life will be like in the forever world.

We must love people as Jesus loved them—without strings attached—and at the same time we must recognize how desperately they need the Savior.

Think with me.

- How does this strike you? Would you say that, in the long run, becoming a follower of Jesus is more or less important than physical and social improvement? On what basis?

- Do you sense a decline in concern about the Christ-transformed eternal life?

- Do you think that approaches to sharing the Gospel must become more subtle and reactive in a world hostile to Christians?

- How can we as church leaders continually reinforce the inestimable importance of spiritual regeneration and life transformation in Christ?

Some Quotes from Others

From David Platt[10]

"Today more than a billion people in the world live and die in desperate poverty. They attempt to survive on less than a dollar per day." "If I am going to address urgent spiritual need by sharing the gospel of Christ or building up the body of Christ around the world, then I cannot overlook dire physical need in the process." (108, 109)

"Caring for the poor is one natural overflow and a necessary evidence of the presence of Christ in our hearts. If there is no sign of caring for the poor in our lives, then there is reason to at least question whether Christ is in our hearts." (110)

"I wonder if followers of Christ 150 years from now will look back at Christians in America today and ask, 'How could they live in such big houses? How could they drive such nice cars and wear such nice clothes? How could they live in such affluence while thousands of children were dying because they didn't have food and water? How could they go on with their lives as though the billions of poor didn't even exist?'" (111)

"Going starts where we live, but it doesn't stop there.... If there are a billion people who have never heard the gospel and billions of others who still have not received the gospel, then we have an obligation to go to them. This is not an option. This is a command, not a calling. What is a matter of calling is where we will go and how long we will stay. We will not all go to the same places, and we will not all stay the same length of time. But it is clearly the will of God for us to take the gospel to the nations." (200)

From Steve Corbett & Brian Fikkert[11]
"The task of God's people is rooted in Christ's mission ... to preach the good news of the kingdom in word and in deed ... particularly ... in spreading the good news among the hurting, the weak, and the poor." (38)

"Poverty is rooted in broken relationships, so the solution to poverty is rooted in the power of Jesus' death and resurrection to put all things into right relationship again." (77)

"The goal is not to make the materially poor all over the world into middle-to-upper-class North Americans, a group characterized by high rates of divorce, sexual addiction, substance abuse, and mental illness. ... The goal is to restore people to a full expression of humanness, to being what God created us all to be, people who glorify God...." (78)

"None of the foundational relationships can experience fundamental and lasting change without a person becoming a new creature in Christ Jesus." "...we cannot hope for the transformation of people without the involvement of the local church and the verbal proclamation of the gospel that has been entrusted to it." (80, 81)

"The goal is for everyone involved to glorify God and enjoy Him forever, not just to increase people's incomes." (95)

"The crucial thing is to help people understand their identity as image bearers, to love their neighbors as themselves, to be stewards over God's creation, and to bring glory to God in all things." (145)

From Christian Buckley and Ryan Dobson[12]
"Christ healed, He fed, He touched, and He loved; but above all, He conquered death and sin to provide an eternal solution to brokenness and separation." (14)

"The hungry need food, but we all need redemption. The blind need sight, but we all need to see our condition and separation from God. Every encounter between God and us has these two dimensions— the physical and the spiritual." (21)

"The focus of Christ's life, as given by His father, was to provide a singular opportunity for whosoever might believe in Him to not perish but have everlasting, reconciled life with Him. This fact is the cornerstone of Scripture. Yet on His way to the cross, Christ invested His life in people." (21)

"On the one hand, we may be tempted to totally abandon social investment in furtherance of the message of salvation and resolutely focus on the pre-eminence of eternity, choosing to center on Christ's death and resurrection and the need for spiritual rebirth. On the other hand, we may be tempted to dilute, if not abandon, the gospel for the achievement of temporal social goods, choosing to focus on Christ's acts of love and call to care for the poor and needy." (25)

"When we define evangelism as just what we say, as a verbal call that requires a response, we improperly segregate it from who we are and what we do. But if we define it just as what we do and segregate it from who Christ is and what He said, then we forget that while Christ existed with people and met their needs, He called for a response. ... We have a Master and He is calling us to live in such a way that the world is evangelized—so that every human is confronted with Christ and offered the chance to accept His sacrifice and surrender to His Lordship." (53)

"No matter what we do in this life to improve our condition or the condition of mankind in general, it will all be rendered meaningless at the last breath of equality, unless what we did reaches into eternity." (59)

"We get it wrong if we say that doing 'good' is 'not good.' ... But we also get it wrong if we don't realize that 'doing good isn't good enough' unless it is tied to eternity." (61)

"We could spend an entire life serving people and never once risk offending anyone. But if we open our mouths and share the biblical gospel of salvation, then we risk offense, humiliation, and scorn. We risk being called unloving, narrow-minded, and intolerant. We risk being persecuted rather than praised. ... Christ opened His mouth and the apostles did the same. The consequences for almost all of them were severe, but if you asked any of them, they would confirm it was worth it. Our evangelism must include what we do and who we are, but it must also include words." (70)

APPENDIX IV:
Make Disciples or Disciple the Nations?

"Make disciples" is *not* the core of the Great Commission. Please don't hear me say that we should not make disciples. We must. In fact, this has been one of our biggest failings, both at home and abroad. We have missed the part of the Great Commission that says "teaching them to obey all I have commanded you." But here's the issue.

Many books on doing church start by stating that the Great Commission is the marching orders for the church. They refer to Matthew 28:19-20, the most common expression of The Great Commission. Open your Bibles and read Matthew 28:19-20. Is this what you read?

"Therefore go and make disciples of all nations, baptizing them in the name of the Father and of the Son and of the Holy Spirit, and teaching them to obey everything I have commanded you. And surely I am with you always, to the very end of the age." (NIV)

Often authors exegete this passage by saying that "Go" is a participle, meaning 'when you go,' or 'as you go,' and the heart of the Great Commission is "make disciples." The author proceeds to write the whole book about how to reach the people in your community. This understanding falls in line with our cultural preoccupation with ourselves: our size, quality, and success. In our nation, more and more of local church income is required to run the church with its growing facilities, multiple staff, and the latest in every kind of equipment. It is analogous to a petroleum refinery that uses almost all the gas it produces to operate the refinery.

We know from grammar school that the irreducible components of a sentence are the subject and the verb. What is the subject in this verse? The subject is an understood "You" (plural). And the main verb is "make." In the case of a transitive verb, one that transfers the action to an object, an object is also required to make a complete sentence. You can't say, "Go call...," without saying "Go call your father," or "Go call the dog." It is incomplete without the object.

So here we have the supposed complete core of the Great Commission, "You make disciples." Or "You (subject), make (verb) disciples (object)." So what's the problem?

The problem is that the word "make" is not in the Greek text. There is no "make" in the sentence. The grammar is better represented in the King James that says, "Go ye therefore and *teach* all nations...." The subject is still "you." But the main verb, a transitive verb, is "teach." The word "teach" might be better understood as "disciple," but perhaps the NIV translators weren't comfortable using the noun "disciple" as a verb, so they translated it "make disciples."

"Teach" and "disciple" are transitive verbs. The thought isn't complete until you name the object. And the object of "teach" is "all nations," (literally, all *the* nations). So the main idea is "You teach (or disciple) all nations." *Thus the core of the Great Commission is not "make disciples" but "disciple all nations."*

The core of the Great Commission is not "make disciples" but "disciple all nations."

There is a great deal of difference between "making disciples" and "discipling all nations." When 'all nations' is reduced to a prepositional phrase, it can easily slip out of our consciousness. The outworking of this in practice is that church leaders focus the overwhelming proportion of church efforts and resources on 'making disciples' of ourselves and people like us nearby but tend to neglect 'all nations.' So churches are busy attracting and converting and teaching people in their churches with relatively little focus on people beyond their communities. And they genuinely understand this as fulfilling The Great Commission.

To show how pervasive is this misunderstanding, I was preparing for a seminar for denomination pastors to which I had given the title, "The Great Commission-Driven Church." One of the pastors organizing the event called me and said, "I have taken training and been doing some teaching on "The Great Commission Church" and I would like to ask you to expand this subject and spend some time talking about global missions."

When a pastor looks at a workshop on the Great Commission and assumes it's going to be locally focused, then it seems that modern writers and church experts have domesticated the Great Commission! And as churches we have fallen right in line.

Let's try to illustrate what this means by means of a story. Let's suppose that my wife is going away for a week to care for her dad. Before she goes, she asks me in a very kind tone, "Honey, you know your folks are coming soon after I get back and since I'm leaving in a hurry, I haven't had time to clean the house. There is one thing I would like you to do while I'm gone. I'd like you to clean the whole house." And knowing I'm often not listening, she continues, "I'd like you to go through the whole house and clean all the rooms." Again, just before she leaves, she sticks her head in my office, gives me a kiss, and says, "Good-by honey. Remember, please clean all the rooms before I get home." "OK," I say as she gets in the car, and I continue working.

As the week goes on, I'm busy. I'm working in my office and occasionally I remember my wife's words, "Clean all the rooms in the house. Clean the house." And I think to myself, "She really wants me to clean up around here." I look around at my messy office and think, "I'd better get busy cleaning." And I start shuffling some papers around and throwing out some accumulated piles of stuff. Later, in my more introspective moments I think to myself again, "She's asking me to clean up." "I've got to clean up." And I throw a little more effort into organizing my office.

I only go in the kitchen to get a bite to eat. I throw the dishes in the sink for later. I only go in the den to watch the news and read a few magazines. I don't even go in the living room. While she's gone I'm terribly busy in the office.

I spend a fair amount of effort cleaning up the office and things look a bit better when one day my wife breezes in the door with a cheery, "Hi, honey, I'm home!" But the smile quickly fades as she looks around the living room with scattered magazines and a half-inch of dust. She walks into the kitchen where the wastebasket is overflowing and the sink is full of dirty dishes. "What happened?" she moans. "What happened to cleaning the whole house?"

You see, there is a big difference between "cleaning up" and "cleaning the whole house." And there is a big difference between "making disciples" and "discipling all the nations." Reaching the world, discipling the nations, is not a program of the church, it is the purpose of the church. And every building, every ministry, and every member are meant to be contributing to that purpose.

APPENDIX V:
Weighed in the Balance:
Balancing Priorities to Achieve
the Church's Purpose

"The Church is engaged in an urgent
global rescue operation."

The ultimate vision is worshiping communities of Jesus' disciples in every context: disciples free from their material, spiritual, physical, and emotional bondages, worshipers who will join those worshiping throngs ultimately in heaven, faith communities of transformed disciples of Jesus.[13]

How does your church need to re-balance to maximize its effectiveness for this vision? Which way do you need to move on the following continua?

- *Mission vs. Everything Else*
  Do we need more mission or is mission too heavily emphasized versus other needs?

- *Prayer vs. Activity*
  Do we need more prayer for mission or more activity in mission?

- *Vertical vs. Horizontal*
  Do we need a more evangelistic emphasis or a more humanitarian emphasis?

- *Internal Focus vs. External Focus*
  Do we need to orient more of our mission experiences to disciple our people or to more effectively accomplish ministry on the field?

- *Long-Term vs. Short-Term*
  Do we need to undertake more mission trips or more long term ministry? Do we need to focus more on quick results or more on the long-term difficult tasks?

- *The World vs. Our Community*
  Do we tend to neglect our community or do we tend to neglect the rest of the world?

- *American Missionaries vs. National Partnerships*
  Do we need to focus more on partnerships with nationals or on sending trained and equipped Americans?

- *Missionaries vs. Projects*
  Do we need to focus more on time-framed projects with defined end points or on supporting long-term workers who can learn the culture and influence people in the long haul?

- *Hands Off vs. Hands On*
  Do we need to deploy more people into hands-on ministry in the world, or are we limiting our long-term effectiveness by excluding ministry where our people can't go help?

- *Continuity vs. Change*
  Are we bound by the past so that we cannot advance, or are we jettisoning the past with too little regard for our rich history and faithful, long-term workers?

- *Strategic Needs vs. Our Interests*
  Are we losing the commitment of our people by focusing
  on strategic needs that are beyond their range of
  understanding and involvement, or are we neglecting
  critical and strategic needs because we limit ourselves to
  the interests of our people?

- *Out of Reach vs. Out of Fellowship*
  Do we neglect those around us who are not believers to do
  international ministry, or do we neglect those out of reach
  of the gospel to put the great majority of our efforts into
  those who have multiplied opportunities already?

How does your church need to rebalance to maximize your
effectiveness in the urgent global rescue operation?

References:
"Six Challenges for the Church in Missions," David Mays, Evangelical
Missions Quarterly, July 2006
"Top Missions Challenges in the Changing U.S. Church," David
Mays, a recorded webinar for The Mission Exchange, Jan 10, 2008

RESOURCES

Bible Study

- *Commissioned*, Marvin J. Newell (Saint Charles, IL: ChurchSmart Resources, 2010)
- *God's Heart for the Nations*, Jeff Lewis (Littleton, CO: Caleb Project, 2002) available from the online store at www.Pioneers.org
- *Mission in the Old Testament*, Walter C. Kaiser Jr. (Grand Rapids, MI: Baker Books, 2000)
- *Missions – God's Heart for the World*, Paul Borthwick (Downers Grove, IL: InterVarsity Press, 2000)
- *Through God's Eyes*, Patrick Cate (Pasadena, CA: William Carey Library, 2004)
- *Until the Whole World Knows*, Alicia Britt Chole (Rogersville, MO: onewholeworld, inc. 2000)

Children

- *Becoming a World Changing Family*, Donna S. Thomas (Grand Rapids, MI: Baker Books, 2004)
- Caleb Project materials. Now a part of Pioneers. See the online store at www.Pioneers.org.
- *Daddy, Are We There Yet?*, Sylvia Foth (Mukilteo, WA: Kidzana Ministries, 2009). A wealth of missions information written as if to children.
- *Window on the World*, Jill Johnstone and Daphne Spraggett (Carlisle, United Kingdom: Paternoster, 2007). A full-color, fascinating prayer guide for unreached peoples.

Compassion Ministries

- *Humanitarian Jesus*, Christian Buckley & Ryan Dobson (Chicago, IL: Moody Publishers, 2010)
- *Just Courage*, Gary A. Haugen (Downers Grove, IL: InterVarsity Press, 2008)
- *The Hole in Our Gospel*, Richard Stearns (Nashville, TN: Thomas Nelson, 2009)
- *Welcoming the Stranger*, Matthew Soerens & Jenny Hwang (Downers Grove, IL: InterVarsity Press, 2009)
- *When Helping Hurts*, Steve Corbett & Brian Fikkert (Chicago, IL: Moody Publishers, 2009)

Conferences, Courses and Consultants

- ACMC Conferences, www.acmc.org
- AERDO Events, Association of Evangelical Relief & Development Organizations, www.aerdo.net
- *Encountering Islam*, a twelve-lesson course combining learning and experience with the Muslim world, www.encounteringislam.org/
- *Kingdom Expansion 101* by Bruce Camp, an online course that provides a biblical and strategic framework to assist churches and individuals in local and global outreach, www.efca.org/reachglobal/reachglobal-ministries/efca-connect/resources/kingdom-expansion-101.
- Missions Fest Conferences. For example, www.missionsfestseattle.org
- Passion Conferences, for college students.
- *Perspectives on the World Christian Movement,* a fifteen-week study of the spread of Christianity in the world, offered at locations throughout the U.S., www.perspectives.org

- *PathWays to Global Understanding,* a thirteen-week journey exploring God's worldwide agenda, www.pathways2.org
- Urbana Student Mission Conference, www.urbana.org
- Webinars (live and recorded) from The Mission Exchange. See the online store at www.TheMissionExchange.org.

Cross-Cultural Relationships Locally and Personally

- "Bridges," Crescent Project, curriculum for building relationships with Muslims, www.crescentproject.org/
- "Cross-Cultural Connections," Mary Lederleitner, 2009. A curriculum on CD for local church groups to learn how to develop relationships with people of other cultures (based on Duane Elmer's book of the same title) Available from the author, mary_lederleitner@wycliffe.net
- *Faces in the Crowd,* Donna S. Thomas (Birmingham, AL: New Hope Publishers, 2008)
- *Serving with Eyes Wide Open,* David Livermore (Grand Rapids, MI: Baker Books, 2006)

Cultural Issues and Cross-Cultural Life and Ministry

- *African Friends and Money Matters,* David Maranz (Dallas, TX: SIL International, 2001)
- *American Cultural Baggage,* Stan Nussbaum, (Maryknoll, NY: Orbis Books, 2005)
- *Cross-Cultural Connections,* Duane Elmer, (Downers Grove, IL: InterVarsity Press, 2002)
- *Cross-Cultural Conflict,* Duane Elmer, (Downers Grove, IL: InterVarsity Press, 1993)
- *Cross-Cultural Servanthood,* Duane Elmer, (Downers Grove, IL: InterVarsity Press, 2006)
- *Leading Across Cultures,* James E. Plueddemann (Downers Grove, IL: InterVarsity Press, 2009)

- *Leading Cross-Culturally*, Sherwood Lingenfelter (Grand Rapids: Baker Academic, 2008)
- *Ministering Cross-Culturally*, Sherwood Lingenfelter (Grand Rapids: Baker, 1986)
- *Miniskirts, Mothers, and Muslims*, Christine A. Mallouhi (Grand Rapids, MI: Monarch Books, 2004)
- *Screams in the Desert*, Sue Eenigenburg (Pasadena, CA: William Carey Library, 2007)
- *Through Her Eyes*, Marti Smith (Waynesboro, GA: Authentic Media, 2004)

Mission Team Operation

- *Becoming a World Changing Church*, David Mays. How to organize your church around the Great Commission, (ACMC, 2006, out of print, access free as a .pdf or purchase from David Mays at www.DavidMays.org)
- *Building Global Minded Christians: A Study of Local Church Mobilization*, Mark Mays, unpublished. Available free at www.davidmays.org/Resources/Building_Global_Minded_ Christians.pdf
- *Building Global Vision: How to Discover God's Mission Vision for Your Church*, David Mays. (ACMC, 2005). Purchase from the online store at www.Pioneers.org.
- *Church Missions Policy Handbook* (ACMC, 3rd ed., 1995). Purchase from the Pioneers online store at www.Pioneers.org.
- *Developing a Missions Strategy that Fits Your Church*, David Mays, 2009, Purchase on CD from David Mays. Much of the material is available free on the web at www.DavidMays.org.
- *How to Operate an Effective Missions Leadership Team in Your Church*, David Mays. (Littleton, CO: Initiative360, 2007) Available from the online bookstore at www.Pioneers.org.
- *Missions in the 21st Century*, Tom Telford (Charlotte, NC: United World Mission, 1998)

- *The Missions Assessment Profile* (ACMC, no date). Available from the online bookstore at www.Pioneers.org
- *Today's All-Star Missions Churches*, Tom Telford (Grand Rapids: MI, Baker Books, 2001)
- *Stuff you need to know about Doing Missions in Your Church*, David Mays (herein referred to as *Stuff*). Five volumes on one CD. An encyclopedia of information relevant to the mission team. Volume I, the contents of each volume, and a cumulative index are available free on the web. Purchase the CD from David Mays at www.DavidMays.org.
- *Your Focus on the World, A Step-by-Step Guide to Leading Your Whole Church into Maximum Global Impact*, Ellen Livingood, www.catalystservices.org

Missionary Care

- Barnabas International, www.barnabas.org
- Global Member Care Network, www.globalmembercare.com
- Missionary Care Resources for Missions and Mental Health, www.missionarycare.com
- *Serving as Senders*, Neal Pirolo (San Diego, CA: Emmaus Road, International, 1991)
- *Tender Care: The Heart and Soul of Caring for God's Scattered Servants*, The Seabrook Seven (Rockford, IL: Barnabas International, 2010)

Missionary Preparation

- *Global Mission Handbook*, Steve Hoke and Bill Taylor (Downers Grove, IL: InterVarsity Press, 2009)
- *Send Me!*, Steve Hoke and Bill Taylor (Pasadena, CA: William Carey Library, 1999)
- "Sending New Missionaries," Ellen Livingood – a packet of downloads for local churches to purchase, www.catalystservices.org/bm~doc/sendnew.pdf

- *Skills, Knowledge, Character: A Church-Based Approach to Missionary Candidate Training,* Greg Carter (Valparaiso, IN: Turtle River Press, 2010) Purchase from TurtleRiverPress@gmail.com
- *To Timbuktu & Beyond: A Guide to Getting Started in Missions,* Marsha Woodard (Pasadena, CA: William Carey Library, 2010)

Partnership

- "About Partnerships and Consortia," ReachGlobal, http://www.efca.org/reachglobal/reachglobal-ministries/efca-connect/partnerships-and-consortia/about-partnerships-and-co
- *Building Strategic Relationships,* Daniel Rickett (Pleasant Hill, CA: Klein Graphics for Partners International, 2000)
- *Cross-Cultural Partnerships,* Mary Lederleitner (Downers Grove, IL: InterVarsity Press, 2010)
- *Making Your Partnership Work,* Daniel Rickett (Enumclaw, WA: WinePress Publishing, 2002)
- *The Beauty of Partnership Study Guide,* Werner Mischke (Scottsdale, AZ, Mission ONE, Inc., 2010). www.beautyofpartnership.org
- *To Give or Not To Give,* John Rowell (Waynesboro, GA: Authentic Media, 2006)
- *When Charity Destroys Dignity,* Glenn Schwartz (Lancaster, PA: World Mission Associates, 2007)
- *Well Connected,* Phill Butler (Waynesboro, GA: Authentic Media, 2006)

Motivation, Encouragement, and Spiritual Growth

- *Don't Waste Your Life,* John Piper (Wheaton, IL: Crossway Books, 2003)
- *Live Life on Purpose,* Claude Hickman (Enumclaw, WA: Pleasant Word, 2003)

- *Living Sacrifice*, Helen Roseveare (Ross-shire, Scotland, UK: Christian Focus Publications, 1980, 2007)
- *Let the Nations Be Glad*, John Piper (Grand Rapids, MI: Baker Academic, 1993, 2010)
- *Radical: Taking Back Your Faith from the American Dream*, David Platt (Colorado Springs, CO: Multnomah Books, 2010)

Prayer

- *Global Prayer Digest*, www.globalprayerdigest.org
- Global Day of Prayer, www.globaldayofprayer.com
- International Day of Prayer for the Persecuted Church, www.persecutedchurch.org
- Muslim Prayer Focus, 30-Days of Prayer for the Muslim World during Ramadan, www.30-days.net
- *Operation World*, Jason Mandryk (Colorado Springs, CO: Biblica, 2010), A strategic prayer guide to the world. See www.operationworld.org. You can also purchase the Operation World CD-ROM, DVD-ROM and wall map from Global Mapping International, www.gmi.org.
- Praying Through the 10/40 Window, www.win1040.com

Special Focus

- Ask a Missionary, www.askamissionary.com
- Business as Mission Network, www.businessasmissionnetwork.com
- Finishers, www.finishers.org
- National Network of Parents of Missionaries, www.pomnet.org
- Unreached Peoples, Joshua Project, www.joshuaproject.org

Trends and Facts

- *Kingdom without Borders*, Miriam Adeney (Downers Grove, IL: InterVarsity Press, 2009)
- *Mission Handbook*, Linda J. Weber, ed., (Wheaton, IL: Evangelism and Missions Information Service, 2010)
- *Operation World, 7th edition*, Jason Mandryk (see above)

Trips

- *Before You Pack Your Bags, Prepare Your Heart*, Cindy Judge (Wheaton, IL: Campfire Resources, 2000), distributed by STEM Press, www.stemintl.org
- Fellowship of Short-Term Mission Leaders, www.fstml.org
- National Short-Term Mission Conference, www.nstmc.org
- *Trip Stuff* by David Mays (on CD). 230 documents mostly developed by local churches covering everything from writing support letters to getting through airports. Purchase from David Mays at www.DavidMays.org.
- "Standards of Excellence in Short-Term Missions," www.stmstandards.org

NOTES

[1] ACMC, Advancing Churches in Missions Commitment, www.ACMC. org, a division of Pioneers, www.pioneers.org

[2] Todd Ahrend, *In This Generation*, (Colorado Springs, CO: Dawson Media, 2010), 307

[3] Ibid., 68

[4] Ibid. 192

[5] Daniel Rickett, *Building Strategic Relationships*, (Pleasant Hill, CA: Klein Graphics for Partners International, 2000), 1

[6] David Hackett and Michael McGill, "Partnership: Equipping the Next Generation for Collaboration," *eXcelerate*, The Mission Exchange, 2010, 14

[7] Steve Hoke and Bill Taylor, *Global Mission Handbook* (Downers Grove, IL: InterVarsity Press, 2009), 158

[8] David Hackett and Michael McGill, 14

[9] Steve Scott, former mission pastor at Midland Evangelical Free Church, Midland, MI, personal communication, August 25, 2010

[10] David Platt, *Radical* (Colorado Springs, CO: Multnomah Books, 2010)

[11] Steve Corbett & Brian Fikkert, *When Helping Hurts* (Chicago, IL: Moody Publishers, 2009)

[12] Christian Buckley and Ryan Dobson, *Humanitarian Jesus* (Chicago, IL: Moody Publishers, 2010)

[13] Steve Hoke and Bill Taylor, *Global Mission Handbook*, (Downers Grove: IL: InterVarsity Press, 2009) 41

ABOUT THE AUTHOR

David Mays, Ph.D.

David Mays is the Director of Learning Initiatives for The Mission Exchange (formerly Evangelical Fellowship of Mission Agencies). Prior to joining The Mission Exchange in 2007, David served more than twenty years as the Great Lakes Regional Director for ACMC, Advancing Churches in Missions Commitment.

Before changing careers in 1983, David worked fifteen years in management for Bristol Myers. He has advanced degrees in both science and theology.

David has been involved in missions all his life as a supporter, layman, church leader, and church consultant. He has helped hundreds of churches to greater missions commitment and effectiveness through workshops, seminars, conferences, consultations, writing, resources, and his website, www.davidmays. org. David has a keen understanding of how to help churches relate missions to contemporary culture. David and his wife, Marcy, live in the Indianapolis area.

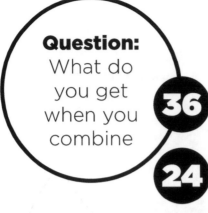

Question: What do you get when you combine

36 **book summaries** *electronically delivered, 3 per month*

24 **live webinars** *average 2 per month*

12 **author interviews** *MP3 downloads, 1 per month*

6 **global issues updates** *bi-monthly downloadable webinar*

3 **and 3 live conferences?**

1 **Answer:** 1 year of member benefits in The Mission Exchange

Connect with The Mission Exchange

THE MISSION
EXCHANGE

Empowering the Global Mission Community

TheMissionExchange.org

〉 Getting Connected

Becoming a church affiliate member of The Mission Exchange will open a door of shared learning, mutual accountability and trusted partnership with other like-minded evangelical mission leaders. You will experience an innovative combination of online resources and live training events designed to add value to church and mission leaders.

The Mission Exchange has been listening to church leaders. Based on their input Church Affiliate Membership has been designed to address three key church issues:

- Church leaders want to help their missionaries stay fresh and growing.
- Church leaders want to help their short-term missionaries continue a journey of world Christian discipleship and keep their vision alive.
- Church decision-makers for missions want to stay in touch with thought leaders and practitioners that have a pulse on what God is doing around the world.

For specific information about how Church Affiliate Membership addresses these specific issues and details about member benefits, visit www.TheMissionExchange.org/churchaffiliate.

We encourage you to consider connecting with The Mission Exchange through church affiliate membership. But it is also possible to participate in training, networking events and live webinars as a non-member.

"I know from personal experience The Mission Exchange is adding value to mission organizations and I'm excited about their commitment to expand these quality services to local churches."
- *Rob Bugh*
Senior Pastor, Wheaton Bible Church